THE DOWNS AND WEALD

GREAT WALKS

THE DOWNS AND WEALD

BARBARA BLATCHFORD
AND CATRIONA MULLIGAN

Photography by John Heseltine

WARD LOCK

Photography by John Heseltine

Text set in 12 on 13pt Linotron Perpetua Roman
by
Tradespools Ltd., Frome, Somerset

Printed and bound in Portugal by Resopal

British Library Cataloguing in Publication Data

Blatchford, Barbara
North and South Downs. – (Great
walks).
1. Kent – visitors' guides
I. Title II. Series
914.22'304858

ISBN 0-7063-6842-8

ACKNOWLEDGMENTS

The Authors acknowledge the support of Surrey County Council. Special thanks are due to our researcher Liz Pamplin, our long suffering families, our many friends who have checked these walks, Peter Turner for help with Barcombe and to all those who have knowingly or otherwise contributed to the book.

CONTENTS

INTRODUCTION

Downs and Weald is the first book in the series of *Great Walks* to be set in lowland Britain and the first which deals with an area which is not a National Park. Some lowland areas were considered for designation following the 1949 National Parks and Access to the Countryside Act, but none in fact was included. However the North and South Downs, and more recently the High Weald, were designated as Areas of Outstanding Natural Beauty. In 1984, the Ministry of Agriculture identified the South Downs as one of only ten Environmentally Sensitive Areas in England and Wales where grants are available to encourage landowners to farm in a traditional way.

In its own way the gentler landscape of the Downs and Weald is as precious a part of our heritage as the wilder upland areas. There is a wide variety of scenery unrivalled by any one National Park. The open chalk Downland contrasts with tree-clad, sandy hills; lowland heath with cereals and orchards and tranquil river valleys with cliffs rising from the sea.

London, with its huge population, is close by and motorways, trunk roads and railways radiate from it. Many people also live in the picturesque towns and villages within commuting distance of the capital. There are pressures on the land but despite this there are still many beautiful and surprisingly quiet areas.

Downs and Weald is threaded with a network of over 12,000 miles (19 200 km) of public footpaths and bridleways. In addition, there is a surprisingly large number of open spaces along the Downs, the Greensand hills, High Weald and the coast, owned by Local Authorities and the National Trust. Here there is freedom to wander without being confined to public paths.

Downs and Weald embraces East and West Sussex and parts of Kent, Surrey and Hampshire. The boundaries used within this book are those of the 'Wealden District' described in the British Regional Geology. The best walking throughout the year is on the Downs and high sandy hills and the majority of the walks visit both their classic viewpoints and the more remote areas. The Low Weald and the coast are not neglected and, although fewer in number, the walks explore different aspects of this varied countryside.

The 24 walks range from $2\frac{1}{2}$ to 27 miles (4 to 43 km) in length and some of the longer ones can be split into shorter circuits giving a total of 28 circular and 2 linear walks. They are divided into four categories, ranging from Easy to More Strenuous and have been carefully chosen to give variety within each category. Many

of the walks can be combined with visits to stately homes, interpretative centres and historic monuments and details are included. All develop aspects of the natural and human history of the area which tell the story of the Downs and Weald, one of the most complex and fascinating areas in Great Britain.

Arable crops at the foot of the Downs.

THE FACE OF THE DOWNS AND WEALD

THE GEOLOGY OF THE DOWNS AND WEALD

The underlying geology of the Downs and Weald has shaped the landscape and provided opportunities and imposed limits on man's use of the area. The complex interaction between man and the landscape in pursuit of food and wealth marks centuries of use and the traditional buildings of the Downs and Weald reflect the changing geology. The flint-clad walls of Downland houses contrast with the sandstones of the Greensand and the High Weald. Clay provided the raw material for tiles and bricks and the large oak trees used to build the timber-framed houses of medieval times grew in the Wealden woods.

The church was the focal point of the local community and frequently the leading families in the parish embellished and added to it reflecting current fashions and whims, but the main building stone was often quarried within the parish.

The geological story of the Downs and Weald began around 135 million years ago when the Wealden clays and sands were laid down in a freshwater lake fed by rivers carrying silt and rock fragments from the surrounding land. Twenty million years later the sea broke into this area and the Lower Greensand, Gault Clay, and then Upper Greensand, were deposited one on top of the other as the sea ebbed and flowed becoming deeper and more extensive. Gradually, the climate became warmer and drier. For

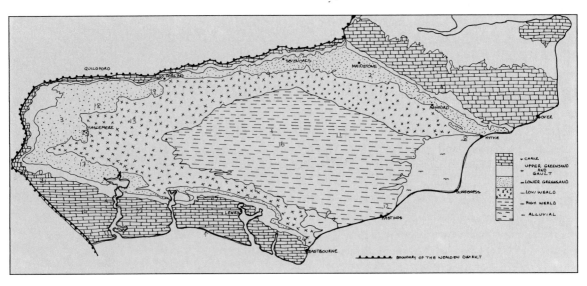

the next 30 million years, with little water in the rivers, the sea was very clear and chalk slowly accumulated on the sea bed as a white sediment made up of fragments of shells and minute marine plants. This soft calcareous mud on the sea floor teemed with an abundance of animal life. Flints in chalk may well have formed from the silicate skeletons of sponges in the sea and many fossils are now found in the chalk. Around 75 million years ago, when the Alps were being formed, there was a gradual folding and uplift of these sediments into a great dome that rose from the sea bed. The Chalk reached its greatest height in the central Weald and weakened by these earth movements fissures opened exposing the older sands and clays. Erosion by wind and rivers slowly removed the overlying Chalk and Greensand to reveal the Wealden rocks. The eroded edges of the Chalk and Greensand are exposed as scarp slopes with gentler dip slopes behind.

The symmetry of the North and South Downs is striking. The steep escarpment of the North Downs in Surrey and Kent faces south overlooking the Greensand hills and the Weald. In Sussex, the escarpment of the South Downs faces north overlooking the less prominent Greensand ridge. The Downs lie on a narrow band of Gault Clay and as rainwater percolates through the Chalk it emerges as a line of springs where it meets the impervious clay at the foot of the scarp. Consequently, there are few older towns and villages on the Chalk but distinct spring line settlements in the fertile valleys.

The arc of the Greensand follows the symmetry of the Downs. In the western Weald a wide belt of Lower Greensand forms picturesque hills culminating in Leith Hill at 948 ft (289 m). Further east the ridge is lower and the soils more fertile.

Within the area, the sandy ridges of Ashdown Forest are surrounded by clay vales. The Chalk, sands and clays combine to form a varied and contrasting landscape.

WOODLAND

After the last Ice Age, the climate began to warm up. Around 8000 BC, sub-Arctic conditions gave way to a more temperate climate and the mosses and lichens of the tundra covering southeast England were colonized by dwarf birch and willow. These, in turn, were followed by birch, pine and hazel and broadleaf woodland gradually spread as oak, lime, elm, ash, and alder became established. Beech, now so characteristic of the Downs, and hornbeam, which grows on the Wealden Clay, followed much later around 6000 BC, shortly before the continental land bridge was submerged and Britain became an island.

Early man, hunting animals and gathering fruits and seeds, had little impact on the woodlands but with Neolithic man, around 4000 BC, there was a gradual change to a more settled agriculture which had a dramatic impact on the landscape in the Downs and Weald. As the Bronze and Iron Age cultures developed, animal rearing became increasingly important. It has been estimated that by 500 BC, the beginning of the Iron Age, 50 per cent of the natural woodland had disappeared over England. For the farmers of this time, the remaining woodlands, which were on the less productive lands, were crucial both for pasturing stock and cutting leaf fodder to be dried and stored for the winter.

Woodland also provided timber for building and coppice for hurdles, wattle fences, tools and fuel. Coppice is produced by cutting trees down almost to ground level every few years. New branches or poles, the underwood, grow from this base or stool.

By the thirteenth century, most of the woodland within the Downs and Weald was managed either as coppice with standards or as wood-pasture. Standards are trees allowed to grow to maturity for timber. In wood-pasture, animals browse beneath widely-spaced standards and pollards. Pollarded trees are cut at a height of 8–12 feet (2.4–3.7 m) and the branches grow up again to produce raised coppice out of reach of browsing animals.

Storm damaged beech.

The lightly populated Low Weald was still heavily wooded in Norman times. Coppice woodland provided a renewable source of raw material for the charcoal burners and charcoal fuelled the developing glass and iron industries. By the Tudor period, there was an increased demand for timber for houses and shipbuilding. Underwood, too, was used for the expanding iron industry. However, the destruction of the Wealden woodlands was probably localized and not as widespread as once believed.

The enclosure awards of the seventeenth to nineteenth centuries led to new plantations of oak and beech and, later, Scots pine. With the gradual collapse of wood-based industries and the use of fossil fuels, many old woodlands became neglected. However, in some areas sweet chestnut was planted and coppiced to produce hop poles and fencing and some of this coppice is still worked and shaped on site in temporary workshops.

Rapid population growth during Victorian times led to Britain becoming largely dependent on softwood imports. During the First World War many plantations were clear felled. This shortage led to the birth of the Forestry Commission in 1919 and then to Government grants and tax relief resulting in a vast increase in coniferous woodland.

Ancient woodland, defined as having been in existence continuously since 1600, is an important habitat for a rich variety of plants and animals. Organizations such as the Woodland Trust

acquire ancient woodlands and are re-introducing traditional management.

A bluebell and wood anemone carpet under an old coppice.

THE GREAT STORM OF 16 OCTOBER 1987

In the early hours of 16 October 1987 gale-force winds swept across south-east England and long before most people had risen from their beds, tiles had been torn from roofs, outbuildings flattened and 15 million trees uprooted. The intensity of the storm increased as it moved eastward across the Downs and Weald and the south-facing slopes and plateau woodlands were the worst affected as the gales blew in from the sea. Destruction was patchy, some woods were scarcely touched while others nearby were flattened. Emergency services swung into action clearing blocked roads and freeing people from their homes. Most woodland paths were blocked and country walks turned into assault courses. The last storm of such ferocity had been in 1703.

By 1989, the majority of paths had been cleared but timber extraction continues. Many uprooted trees will remain where they fell, gradually decaying and providing a haven for the numerous invertebrates and fungi which live on dead wood.

The Wealden harvest.

While creating havoc and financial loss, the 1987 storm has provided an opportunity for renewal. Many of the oaks and beeches which fell were over-mature trees of neglected woodlands and the opening out of the canopy not only creates new views but allows young trees, both those present before the storm and new plantings, to grow to delight future generations. With increased light, bluebells, wood anemones and primroses flourish in a manner not seen since the underwood was coppiced regularly. While some woods were devastated and clear felling and insensitive timber extraction have destroyed a few valuable woodlands, many others have been revitalized.

COMMONS AND ENCLOSURES

The history of land use is written in today's landscape and no-where is this truer than on the commons. Commoners' rights have existed from time immemorial and they formed an integral part of the manorial system established by the Normans. The commons, or manorial wastes, were owned by the Lord of the Manor but the tenants had certain rights in common and these were limited and regulated by the Manorial Courts. Details varied between manors, but generally there was a right to pasture swine, cattle and sheep; cut turf or peat; to fish, and to cut the under-wood for fencing, farm implements and firewood. On heathland, bracken was cut for bedding and furze and old heather gathered for fuel. The timber trees, sporting and mineral rights belonged to the Lord of the Manor.

Commons varied. On sandy soils, there were extensive tracts of heathland, whereas grassland prevailed on more fertile soils and other areas were wooded.

William the Conqueror introduced forests into England. A medieval forest was not a heavily wooded area but land on which deer were protected. The Royal Hunting Forests and the smaller Deer Parks to which every magnate aspired, were protected by Forest Laws and surrounded by a park pale, that is, a bank with a fence on top and an internal ditch so that deer could easily leap into the area but only escape with difficulty. Commoners still exercized their rights on common land within the pale.

The seventeenth century saw the invention of new farm machinery and the introduction of new crops such as potatoes and turnips which could grow on poorer soils. The Agricultural Revolution was underway! Landowners wished to obtain greater profit from the common land and to surround their country houses with landscaped parkland. Some common land had been enclosed during medieval times but it was the economic and social pressures leading to the Enclosure Acts of 1607–1876 which had such a profound effect on the landscape. The En-closure Commissioners had to allow sufficient common land to remain to satisfy what they considered to be the needs of the commoners. Boundary banks can be found in woodlands and along field edges. A few are ancient, many undatable, and some relate to these enclosure awards.

Today's commons are the remnants of a pre-enclosure land-scape but the majority look very different from when the land around them was first enclosed. Most commoners' rights are at-tached to the property, but they can, and often have been, bought by the landowner. However, few of the remaining rights are now exercized. Grazing declined and virtually ceased during this century and, increasingly, common land is reverting to woodland.

Local Authorities and the National Trust now own many commons and they are managed to strike a balance between conservation and access.

THE DOWNS

The smooth contours of the Downs are broken by hillforts, barrows, old field systems and quarries and embellished by the curious art of cutting figures in the Chalk. The Downs are characterized by dry valleys which are thought to have been formed by summer meltwater during the last Ice Age. The intersection of the North and South Downs with the sea creates imposing Chalk cliffs at Dover and Beachy Head with the dry valleys between the Seven Sisters hanging high above the sea.

There are differences between the North and South Downs. Large areas of the North Downs are capped by peri-glacial clay with flints supporting woodlands, but the South Downs are more open as there is much less cover by these superficial deposits.

Over the centuries, Chalk grassland developed on the Downs in response to sheep grazing. It was the Neolithic farmers who first introduced grazing animals and by the eighteenth century the Downs had been grazed by sheep for some 5000 years. The sheep were grazed on the open Downland during the day and taken down to the lower fields at night. At different times of the year they were folded or grazed on cereal stubble and the home pasture and their droppings fertilized this land. This well-balanced and integrated approach developed over the centuries producing wool, mutton and sheep skins. The economic importance of the medieval wool industry is symbolized today by the Lord Chancellor's woolsack in the House of Lords. Although there was little thought for nature conservation, the constant nibbling by sheep produced a short springy downland turf with an intricate mixture of plants.

Surprisingly, it is the poor quality of the thin soil overlying the chalk that is responsible for this diversity. The more vigorous plants are kept in check by constant grazing, allowing others to flourish. Some plants, such as chalk milkwort, are now confined to old Downland but best-known are the beautiful orchids which flower from May through to September in the Downland turf. Rapid growth of aggressive species of grasses is controlled both by grazing and low levels of phosphates and nitrates. Large numbers of insects, especially butterflies, depend on the flowers for their survival. The attractive chalk hill and common blues need short turf on steep slopes to breed and the caterpillars of the vivid black and red burnet moth feed on bird's foot trefoil and clovers. The bulky ant hills of the yellow meadow ant are good indicators of undisturbed Downland.

Downland went under the plough to produce cereals both before and after the Napoleonic wars but it gradually reverted as the economic climate changed. Many acres, especially on the South Downs, again fell to the plough this century during the two World Wars. In other areas, Downland was simply abandoned. Until 1953, with the introduction of myxomatosis, grazing rabbits, brought across the Channel by the Normans and harvested from warrens during medieval times, helped to keep invading scrub in check. But since their numbers were decimated, the invasion of chalk grassland has accelerated.

Unless the chalk grassland of the Downs and Weald is actively managed, many of the plants and animals associated with it will eventually disappear. The Nature Conservancy Council and the National Trust have been instrumental in reintroducing sheep grazing to conserve small oases of plants and animals which were once far more widespread.

THE GREENSAND AND THE HIGH WEALD

In the eastern Weald, alternate bands of sandy limestone and calcareous sandstone, the Rag and Hassock of the Hythe beds, have been quarried over the centuries for building stone. They give rise to light, fertile soils on which acres of apples, cherries and soft fruit are grown.

In the west, cherty sandstones make up the Hythe beds and form the highest hills of the Downs and Weald with their acid, infertile soils. The younger calcareous Bargate beds are quarried for building stone and, like the Rag and Hassock, support fertile soils.

Large quantities of building sand and ironstone are extracted from the Folkestone beds. Many older buildings are decorated with small fragments of ironstone set into the mortar between the sandstone blocks. This is known locally as galetting.

Like chalk grassland, the large tracts of heathland that once covered the high sandy hills of the western Weald and the Ashdown Forest were created by man and the fragmentary remains, now isolated from the economic system that sustained them, need careful management and protection if they are to survive. The farmers of the Neolithic, Bronze and Iron Ages cleared large areas of broadleaf woodland but the acid, sandy soils could only support crops and pasture for a short time and so heather, gorse and bracken gradually spread. The impoverished soil, with an

A weatherboarded oast house near Goudhurst.

upper layer of leached nutrients and a thin band of humus and iron deposited beneath, favours the heathland plants, but without grazing, woodland soon invades.

By Roman times, many heaths already existed. Although some may have reverted to woodland following the Roman exodus, the majority were maintained by the Saxons and then their Norman conquerors and incorporated into their manorial system. The heaths left as common land were not desolate or barren but a vital part of the economy. The combined effect of the enclosures awards, new plantations and commoners no longer exercizing their rights means that it is now only possible in the Ashdown Forest and the Frensham–Thursley area to get some impression of what the many vast tracts of heathland must have looked like. Elsewhere woodland has invaded the once open heaths.

The characteristic heathland plants ranging from heathers and gorse to the rare marsh gentian support many species of insects and spiders. Heathland is the home of the increasingly rare sand lizards and smooth snakes and birds such as the nightjar and a dartford warbler. Without active management the lowland heaths will not survive. Most are now designated Sites of Special Scientific Interest but increased leisure time adds to the pressure on heathland and to the problem of reconciling access with the conservation of these fragile areas.

RIVERS

The pattern of the rivers in the Downs and Weald is perverse. Instead of following the line of least resistance – parallel to the Downs – the major rivers have cut deep gaps through them to reach the River Thames or the English Channel. This can be traced back to the geological dome forming their watershed. The River Mole has cut a dramatic gap through the North Downs with a steep river cliff rising up to Box Hill above, whereas the Ouse meanders through a much wider gap in the South Downs.

None of the rivers lent themselves naturally to canalization. In any event, a great deal of opposition to the idea was experienced from mill owners. They were reluctant for the water to be diverted to operate locks despite the fact that from 1600 onwards, various Acts of Parliament had been passed to make some of the rivers navigable. Many schemes were planned but few were executed. The river Ouse in Sussex was made navigable between Lewes and Lindfield in 1800 and in Surrey in 1816 the Wey–Arun canal was built linking London to the south coast to extend the Thames trade. However, with the exception of the Wey and Godalming navigations, none achieved prosperity because there was insufficient industry. The navigations helped local trade and agriculture but with the coming of the railways there was a rapid decline.

The Coast

Erosion and deposition, that unending geological theme, is everywhere in evidence along the south-east coast. The North Downs rise sheer from the sea at Dover and the South Downs end dramatically at Beachy Head. Close inspection reveals cracks in the cliffs and rock debris from cliff falls scattered along the beach. This story is repeated where sandstone cliffs meet the sea. Constant battering, coupled with landslips caused by the sandstone sliding over the slippery clay exposed at the foot of the cliffs, leads to continual erosion. Near Hastings parts of the cliff-top path have been closed for fear of new landslips.

At Romney Marsh the recent geological story is one of deposition. Shingle bars were laid down by the easterly sea currents and the silting up of the estuaries behind them allowed Romney Marsh to emerge from the sea. The construction of sea walls and drainage of the area from Roman times onwards accelerated this process. The Greensand cliffs of an ancient shoreline rise steeply behind the now dry marsh. The stranded ruins of the Roman forts of the Saxon shore and the landlocked Cinque ports of Romney and Winchelsea bear witness to the change.

Romney Marsh and the surrounding levels protected by sea walls are below high water mark. It is this area and the many coastal resorts which will be under the greatest threat if predicitions about the 'greenhouse' effect prove to be true when a rising sea will again reclaim the land.

INTRODUCTION TO THE ROUTE DESCRIPTIONS

1. ACCESS (see page 187)

All the walks follow public rights of way and some also cross open spaces and nature reserves. The majority of these open spaces are owned and managed by County and District Councils or the National Trust. Most nature reserves are owned or managed by the Nature Conservancy Council, a government body, or by voluntary organizations such as the County Naturalist Trusts.

2. STARTING AND FINISHING POINTS

Most of the walks start and finish at public car-parks or car-parks on open spaces. The location of each is described and the six figure grid reference that follows pinpoints the car-park and refers to the relevant Ordnance Survey Pathfinder map. Please park with consideration for others. The police advice is to take all valuables with you or leave them at home.

Two of the walks rely on public transport for the outward or return journey. Details are given with each of these walks. Most of the circular walks can be reached using public transport, if not at the start, then at some point on route. Services change but Tourist Information Centres can help.

Below: *The Downs and Weald. The numbers indicate the approximate starting points for the routes described.*

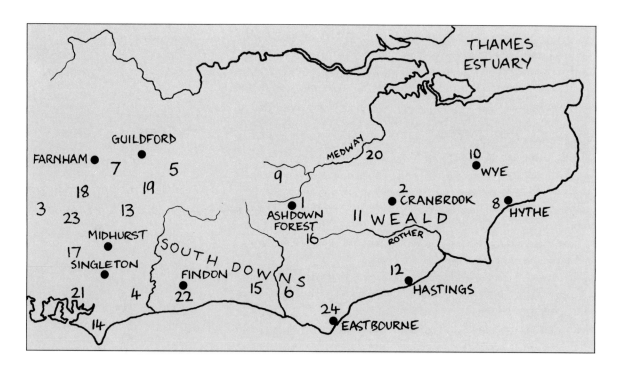

3. LENGTH — The length of each walk has been measured from the relevant Ordnance Survey Pathfinder map. No attempt has been made to take into account any ascent or descent.

4. TIME FOR COMPLETION — Experienced walkers will be able to estimate the length of time to suit their own pace but speed of walking is a very individual matter and anyone unsure of how fast they might travel should work on a speed of not more than 2 miles (3.2 km) per hour. This does not take into account the time needed for rests, food and visiting places of interest.

5. ASCENT — The amount of ascent has been estimated from the Ordnance Survey Pathfinder map and is approximate only. This is one of the factors which has been taken into account when ranking the walks.

6. ROUTE DESCRIPTION — The routes are described in detail but not every gate and stile is mentioned. In any event, it must be remembered that the countryside is undergoing constant change and fences, gates and stiles can be removed and new ones erected. However, by using the map and looking ahead for the next feature this should not be a problem. The word 'track' is used to describe a wide grassy or stony route whereas 'path' describes a narrower, less obvious way, irrespective of whether they are footpaths or bridleways.

Several of the longer walks can be divided into two or more circuits and this is clearly described in the margin.

The majority of the walks are along well-defined paths and tracks on the Downs or Greensand hills but some inevitably cross farmland where changes to the route descriptions are likely to be the greatest. For example, pasture may change to arable and paths may not be reinstated after ploughing. Some potential problems have been noted in the text.

7. ABBREVIATIONS USED IN ROUTE DESCRIPTIONS

L	left
R	right
Half L/R	45 degree turn
Bear L/R	direction varies between almost straight ahead to almost a right angle and is used in association with a feature on the ground
OS	Ordnance Survey
SSSI	Site of Special Scientific Interest
NNR	National Nature Reserve
NT	National Trust

8. INTERESTING FEATURES ALONG THE ROUTE — Their location is indicated both in the route desctions and on the maps by the figures 1, 2, etc and a short description follows. A

number of walks pass houses, windmills and parks which have limited opening times and many are shut in the winter. Details can be obtained from Tourist Information Centres.

9. MAPS   The maps accompanying the route description are drawn to a scale of 1:25 000. Relevant Ordnance Survey Pathfinder maps are indicated for each walk. The maps have been drawn in accordance with the style set by the rest of the series so that the direction of travel is generally from the bottom to the top of the page. The north point is shown on each map by an arrow. Where the walk can be divided into shorter circuits this is marked on the maps by the letters A, B, etc, and keyed into marginal notes.

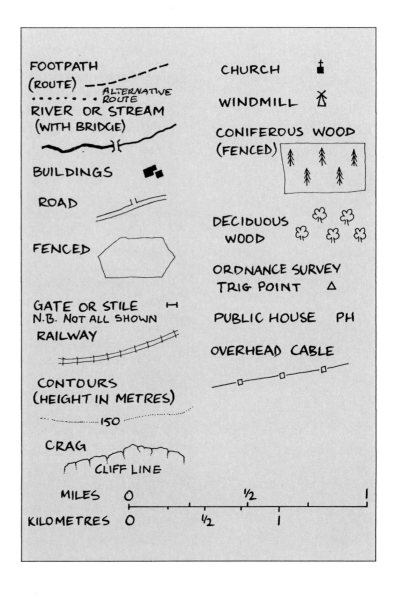

10. THE WALKS

These walks range in length from $2^1/_2$ miles (4 km) to 27 miles (44 km) and, as previously described, some of the longer ones can be divided into shorter circuits.

All the walks can be undertaken at any time of the year. Boots are not essential in the summer but they do give support to the ankles. All footwear must have good patterned soles for grip. Wet chalk particularly can be very slippery and boots or wellingtons will be needed on clay after wet weather. The South Downs can be surprisingly exposed, and warm, windproof clothing should be carried on all but the hottest days. Many walks pass public houses and shops but drink and some food should always be carried.

Each of the walks has been given a grading based on its length, amount of ascent and the nature of the terrain. Generally, walks within these grades will be as follows:

Easy (1) Short walks under 5 miles (8 km) on well-defined paths or tracks.

Moderate (2) Rather longer walks up to about 11 miles (18 km) and generally with more ascent. Some of the walks are on the Low Weald and these route descriptions are more intricate.

More Strenuous (3) Longer walks between 11 and 20 miles (18 and 29 km) in length, which are generally hilly. Most have short steep ascents but the route finding is no more difficult than for the Moderates.

Very Strenuous (4) These two are over 20 miles (32 km) in length but they can be completed comfortably in one day by strong walkers.

11. LONG DISTANCE PATHS

Several Long Distance Paths and Bridleways traverse the Downs and Weald and where a walk meets and leaves them this is noted in the route description using their initials.

Downs Link (DL) This Long Distance Bridleway runs for 30 miles (48 km) across the western end of the Weald, linking the North Downs Way at St Martha's Hill to the South Downs Way near Steyning. Most of the route follows the trackbeds of disused railways and was developed by Waverley Borough Council, West Sussex County Council and Surrey County Council. It is way-marked with green and white discs.

Greensand Way (GW) The Surrey Greensand Way runs for 55 miles (89 km) across the Greensand hills from Haslemere in the west to Limpsfield Chart in the east. Here it joins the Kent section of the route which follows the Greensand ridge for 50 miles (80 km) across the county to meet the Saxon Shore Way near Hamstreet. The routes were devized by members of the

Ramblers' Association and the Surrey section has since been developed as a recreational route by the County Council. The route is waymarked with discs and arrows with GW inscribed.

North Downs Way (NDW) The North Downs Way is a National Trail. It runs for 141 miles (227 km) from Farnham eastwards along the Downs of Surrey and Kent to Dover. At Boughton Lees in Kent there is a choice of route, the direct one going over Wye Downs to Folkestone and then along the cliffs to Dover, while the alternative goes to Dover via Canterbury. The route is waymarked throughout with white acorns and by wooden NDW signposts in Surrey and concrete markers in Kent.

Saxon Shore Way (SSW) The Saxon Shore Way is a Long Distance Path developed by members of the Ramblers' Association and waymarked in places by concrete slabs bearing a red-horned Viking helmet. It runs for over 135 miles (216 km) from Gravesend in Kent to Rye in Sussex along a route approximating to an ancient shoreline.

South Downs Way (SDW) This National Trail runs for 80 miles (129 km) along the South Downs from Eastbourne across Sussex to Hampshire. Between Eastbourne and Alfriston there is an alternative footpath route following the coastal path. It is waymarked throughout with white acorns and by wooden SDW signposts and concrete markers.

Sussex Border Path (SBP) This 150-mile (241 km) route developed by members of the Ramblers' Association follows public rights of way approximating to Sussex's border with Hampshire, Kent and Surrey. There is also a mid-Sussex link following the administrative boundary separating East and West Sussex. It is partially waymarked with wooden SBP signposts.

Vanguard Way (VW) This route, developed by the Vanguards Rambling Club, runs from the suburbs at Croydon for 63 miles (101 km) across the Downs and Weald to the coast at Seaford. It is not waymarked.

Weald Way (WW) The Weald Way is an 80-mile (129 km) footpath running from the Thames at Gravesend across the Downs and Weald to Eastbourne on the south coast, linking the North Downs Way to the South Downs Way. It was developed and waymarked by members of the Ramblers' Association with the support of County and District Councils.

1·1

TOP OF ASHDOWN FOREST

STARTING AND FINISHING POINT
Ashdown Forest Four Counties car-park, on the west side of the B2026 just south of the junction with the B2110. 3 miles (4.8 km) south-east of Forest Row (TQ 43/53–467313).
LENGTH
2 ½ miles (4 km)
ASCENT
230 ft (70 m)
The route joins and leaves walk 3.16 (Ashdown Forest and Wythiam) at points A and B respectively.

This short, scenic walk starts near the highest point in the Ashdown Forest where there is a feeling of openness and space quite different from anywhere else in the Weald. Visitors are attracted to the many car-parks lining the central roads and a weekday visit is recommended when it is possible to gain some impression of the remoteness of the area before the invasion of the motor car. In dry weather there is a significant fire risk in this area. Please DO NOT light fires or drop cigarettes or matches.

ROUTE DESCRIPTION (Map 1)

Go to far end of car-park to visit the Four Counties Dial which identifies the views over the extensive open area of the Ashdown Forest *(1)* and across the Weald to five hills visited on other walks. Return to car-park entrance and cross road to small path opposite. Turn R along very wide track. Turn L up broad track opposite next car-park (Shadows). Go over cross-track. Turn R immediately before the group of pine trees surrounded by a bank. This is Greenwood Gate clump *(2)*, at 732 feet (223 m), the highest point in the Ashdown Forest.

Turn L on wide track, go over diagonal cross-track then bear L alongside pines and keep ahead on well-defined path between gorse. Pass two very small ponds on R which provide a haven for dragonflies and other insects, then, 20 yards (18 m) before Y-junction, turn L down small path. Go over cross-path and continue downhill. Gills Lap Clump can be seen on the hilltop ahead.

Cross footbridge in valley bottom and go uphill. The path can be muddy near the stream where clay is exposed. Near top, keep ahead to go around edge of wood on R and bear L up to road. Go straight across Piglets car-park, over sleeper bridge and uphill on path. Turn L up broad track. To visit the Enchanted Place *(3)* bear R to memorial tablet and view-point surrounded by chestnut fencing. Return to track.

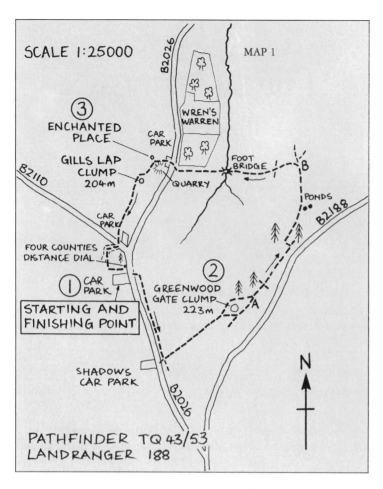

Continue uphill, pass old quarry on L where Ashdown sand-stone can be seen and keep ahead to go to the R of Gills Lap clump and follow wide track along and downhill. Pass to R of young conifer plantation and Gills Lap car-park. Cross road and go up No Through Road. In 35 yards (32 m), where road bears R, turn L up path through heather. Turn L up path to lone pine, Four Counties Dial, and car-park.

1 The Ashdown Forest

The Ashdown Forest, at least in historic times, has never been ploughed. In 1372, Edward III granted the heath and wood-land to his third son John of Gaunt, Duke of Lancaster, and for nearly 300 years Lancaster Great Park, as it was called, was a Royal Hunting Forest.

During the turbulent times of the Civil War, deer were plundered from the park, wood was cut illegally and ore

The view from Gill's Lap across the Weald to the North Downs.

extracted for the local iron industry. After the restoration of Charles II in 1660 he leased it to the Earl of Dorset, a member of the Sackville family, who allowed 'improvers' to enclose areas of the forest for agriculture much to the annoyance of the commoners who retaliated by breaking down fences and trampling crops. In 1693, an enclosure award authorized the enclosure of over half of the Forest leaving 6400 acres (2590 hectares) for common grazing. This is the present Ashdown Forest.

The 1974 Ashdown Forest Act gave the public a right of access on foot over the whole Forest. It also gave the management of the Forest to a board of Conservators made up of elected commoners and local Council Members.

2 *The Clumps*
Eight groups of Scots pine, each surrounded by a boundary bank, were planted on the heights of Ashdown Forest by Arabella Diana, Lady of the Manor of Duddleswell in 1825. Two of these, Greenwood Gate and Gills Lap, are visited on this walk. She granted the public the right to visit the clumps and this was the only public right-of-access over much of the Forest until the 1974 Act.

3 *The Enchanted Place*
'And by and by they came to an enchanted place on the very top of the Forest called Galleons Lap' wrote the author of Winnie the Pooh who lived nearby at Cotchford farm. A memorial tablet commemorates AA Milne (1882–1956) and his illustrator EH Shepherd 'who collaborated in the creation of Winnie the Pooh and so captured the magic of Ashdown Forest and gave it to the world.'

1·2

LINTON AND BOUGHTON MONCHELSEA

STARTING AND FINISHING
POINT
Park in lay-by 200 yards (180 m)
south of church on the east side of
the A229 in the village of Linton
(TQ 65/75–755500).
LENGTH
4 miles (6.5 km)
ASCENT
175 ft (50 m)

The medieval lych gate at St Peter's Church, Boughton Monchelsea.

This walk lies within the 'Garden of England' and is especially recommended in spring when the fruit orchards are in full bloom. It passes two fine country houses set in a magnificent position on the crest of the Greensand ridge overlooking the Weald.

ROUTE DESCRIPTION (Map 2)

From the lay-by turn R up the road and then turn R again up steps joining GW. Go through the churchyard, keeping church on L. Leave through kissing gate and follow path which crosses drive to Linton House *(1)*. Keep ahead on enclosed path, cross road and follow track alongside orchards and soft fruit. Just before road, turn L on path parallel to road, or to visit Boughton Monchelsea Place and church *(2)* keep ahead. Return to route.

Cross road and follow path ahead then bear R over field used for car-parking. Go over drive, the main access to house, and keep ahead between fields. At end of second field, just before gate, turn R down field edge leaving GW. Half way down second field turn L over stile and R along field edge. Look for stile to turn R back through hedge and over stream. Bear L across parkland a little way from woodland edge to causeway over stream with views up to Boughton Monchelsea house. Bear R over field up to stile in field corner and keep ahead up road.

27

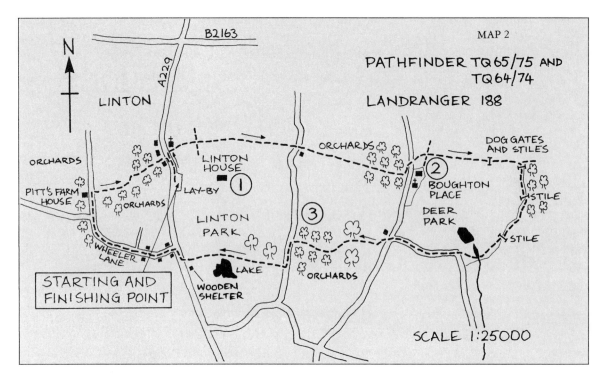

At T-junction turn L and then R along field edge beyond house. At field corner turn R over ditch and L beside it to follow path through woodland and orchards *(3)* to road. Turn L along road and in 75 yards (70 m) turn R on path beside wire fence. Keep ahead through parkland to pass pond on L and bear R towards wooden shelter and road. Turn R along pavement and then L along Wheeler Lane. At Pitts Farm House turn R along field edge. At end of hedge turn L then R up through orchard and up enclosed path to road. Turn R down road back to lay-by.

1 Linton House
In 1730, Robert Mann built this splendid house in an elevated position overlooking the wide sweep of the Weald. By 1829, Thomas Cubbit, Belgravia's architect, had added a third storey, a fine terrace and a central portico overlooking the formal gardens. A ha-ha with a stone retaining wall separates the grazing animals in the parkland from the gardens without interrupting the view from the house. Stuccoed and painted white, the house would not look out of place on the Riviera.

2 Boughton Monchelsea Place and St Peter's Church
St Peter's parish church lies between the garden of Boughton Monchelsea Place and its deer park where a herd of fallow deer still roam. The church is framed by the medieval lych gate and on the verge opposite, the upper stone of a mounting block bears the date 1717.

A sea of bluebells and dog's mercury under an old coppice.

Apple blossom near Linton.

Boughton Monchelsea Place is another fine mansion built on the crest of the Greensand ridge. Part of the village's unusual name comes from the Saxon word Bocton meaning a clearing in a beech wood. At the end of the twelfth century the manor came into the possession of the Norman Montchensies. In 1551 the manor was bought by Robert Rudstone who was largely responsible for its rebuilding using local Kentish Rag stone. Five stone mullion windows are all that remain of the original medieval hall house which faced the church. The present village grew up around the Boughton quarries, which supplied stone to Westminster Abbey.

3   *Orchards*

The close proximity to London and the development of the railways in the mid-1800s nurtured the 'Garden of England' providing an insatiable market for the produce of Kent's orchards and market gardens. Apples with delightful names such as Cox's Orange Pippin, Russet and Worcester Pearmains, cherries and soft fruit have flowed and continue to do so into the capital.

New varieties of apples such as Golden Delicious have also been introduced and many acres of soft fruit and salad vegetables are now grown under huge nylon sheets which envelop the fields during the germination and early growing season. Today, the traditional, tall apple ladders are no longer needed because with new dwarfing root stocks the older standard trees have been replaced with neat, trim orchards.

Despite the new technology, the loss of pollinating bees and wasps would have serious consequences for fruit growers. It is expensive and not always practical to import bee hives.

FRENSHAM COUNTRY PARK

STARTING AND FINISHING POINT
Frensham Little Pond car-park, signed off the A287, 2 miles (3.2 km) south of Farnham (SU 84/94–859418).
LENGTH
4 miles (6.4 km)
ASCENT
200 ft (60 m)

The reed beds at Frensham Little Pond.

This attractive walk on sandy tracks across south-west Surrey's heathland is especially recommended in late summer when the heather is in bloom and studded with patches of yellow gorse. In dry weather there is a significant fire risk in this area. Please DO NOT light fires or drop cigarettes or matches.

ROUTE DESCRIPTION (Map 3)

Keep ahead through car-park parallel to road on L. Go through staggered barrier ahead across grass and step over barrier to road. Immediately bear R on parallel sandy path. Turn R through barrier and keep ahead around Little Pond *(1)*. Some 100 yds (90 m) beyond fence corner turn R through gap and along track with pond on R. Cross causeway and immediately turn R on narrow path through trees and around pond. At pond corner go over wide sandy track. Bear L on track and then turn R up to top of Kings Ridge *(2)*.

Turn L to go along path to R of, and parallel to, broad sandy track. 30 yards (27 m) after staggered barrier, bear R down sandy path. Turn R on cross-path down to road with the obelisk recording the gift of the common to the NT away to the R.

Cross road and turn R around the Great Pond *(3)* and then bear L between fences. Keep ahead with entrance to car-park on R. Go through staggered barrier and straight ahead up R of two sandy tracks with Ranger's office/toilets and second car-park on far L. Go over small cross-track and at five-way junction go straight ahead. Turn R on cross-track up to higher land with Great Pond below on R. At T-junction in front of pine woodland, bear R downhill and turn L to road. Cross and keep ahead up track to top of ridge, briefly meeting outward route. Bear slightly L to go downhill on path towards Little Pond. Bear L on track and keep ahead over cross-track alongside Little Pond. At five-way junction, turn R and near far end of pond bear L to follow path past building on R back to car-park.

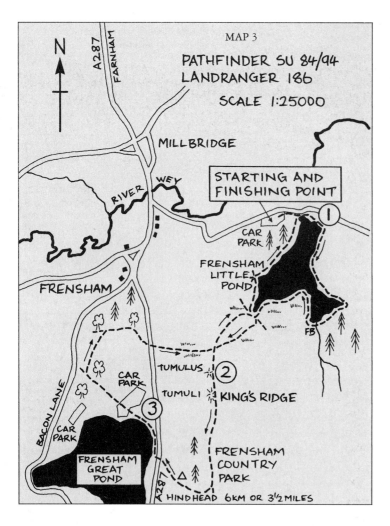

MAP 3

PATHFINDER SU 84/94
LANDRANGER 186

SCALE 1:25000

N

A287 FARNHAM

MILLBRIDGE

WEY
RIVER

STARTING AND
FINISHING POINT

CAR
PARK

①

FRENSHAM
LITTLE
POND

FRENSHAM

FB

TUMULUS ②
TUMULI KING'S RIDGE

CAR
PARK

BACON LANE

③

CAR
PARK

FRENSHAM
GREAT
POND

FRENSHAM
COUNTRY
PARK

A287

HINDHEAD 6KM OR 3½ MILES

1 Frensham Country Park and Little Pond

Frensham Country Park is owned by the NT and managed by Waverley Borough Council. It became a Country Park in 1971 and has for many years been a popular place for visitors from the surrounding areas. The major attractions are the Great and Little Ponds where the Folkestone beds of the Lower Greensand provide an ideal beach closer for some than the coast. South-west Surrey's heathlands, which developed on these infertile sandy soils, are of prime importance for nature conservation and have been designated SSSIs. The commons are relics of the pre-enclosure landscape of medieval England and, until recently, commoners exercizing their rights to pasture animals and cut bracken and wood maintained the virtually treeless landscape of this heathland allowing unique plant and

Frensham Little Pond.

animal communities to develop which cannot now live else-where. Both smooth snakes and sand lizards, which need insects living on old heather for food and bare undisturbed areas of sand in which to lay their eggs, are now virtually confined to the lowland heath. The open heath provides shelter for a wide variety of spiders and sand-burrowing bees and wasps.

The open heath has become invaded by birch and Scots pine and the heather is shaded out and each year Conservation Volunteers take part in 'pine pulls' to help maintain the heath-land. Fire is a great hazard as uncontrolled burning destroys wildlife and creates a desert in which little but bracken sur-vives. Swathes of heather are mown to encourage the growth of young shoots on which particular insects and spiders live.

Important features of the occasional patch of wet heath-land, which develops where drainage has been impeded, are the rare marsh gentian with its blue trumpet-like flower appearing in late summer and the dragonflies and damselflies breeding in the water. Sundew plants which trap and digest unsuspecting insects in their sticky leaves are also found in these wet areas.

The Little Pond was created in 1246 to supply fish to the Bishops of Winchester who lived in Farnham Castle lying to the north. Together with the Great Pond it has considerable wildlife interest, often holding large numbers of wintering duck. Dogs and people are kept well away from the Little Pond's SW corner by a moat dug to protect the reed beds.

2 Kings Ridge

The Kings Ridge commands a superb view over these heath-lands. A line of four bowl barrows along the ridge, now scarcely visible, clearly indicates that the area had been cleared of trees as long ago as the Bronze Age.

Only 148,258 acres (60,000 hectares) of lowland heathland remains in Britain and 9.8 per cent of this is found in Surrey. There are very few large areas of this habitat left in Europe. The remaining areas need both protection and careful manage-ment to prevent bracken, young pines and birch from shading out the fragile heather.

3 The Great Pond

The Great Pond covers the site of a natural pool which was fed by a spring rising near Churt to the south. The pond was prob-ably extended before 1208 by building an embankment which imprisoned streams from Hindhead and Whitmoor Bottom on the south-west side. To prevent silting, the inlet was con-trolled by an elaborate system of ditches and sluices. A trench was constructed around the west side of the pond so that it could be drained and the fish taken out.

Frensham Country Park with its bell heather, ling and scrub oak.

1·4

BIGNOR HILL

STARTING AND FINISHING
POINT
NT car-park at the top of Bignor
Hill. Follow the signs to Bignor
Roman Villa off the A285 south of
Petworth or the A29 at Bury. Pass
the entrance to the villa on R then,
at offset crossroads, turn L past
farm and up narrow lane to car-
park (SU 81/91–974130).
LENGTH
4 miles (6.5 km)
ASCENT
450 ft (140 m)

Ideally this short route starting from the crest of the South
Downs should be walked on a clear day to enjoy the extensive
panoramas but the firm tracks over farm and woodland provide
good walking at any time of year.

ROUTE DESCRIPTION (Map 4)

Stand by signpost with back to car-park. Go ahead and turn L
along chalk track with a view to the L along the escarpment of the
Downs to the clump of trees on Chanctonbury Hill. Follow track
over cross-track and ahead downhill.

250 yards (228 m) before flint cottage turn R up broad cross-
track and follow along, then up through woods. At wood edge
turn R then L along fenced track to go into badly storm-damaged
woods. Turn L along cross-track and go across field from where
splendid views open out towards the south coast and the windmill on Halnaker Hill can be seen away to the R.

Continue on fenced path downhill between fields *(1)*. At end
of second field, turn R on path almost opposite stile on L then turn
R at T-junction. Ignore track to L and keep ahead up path past
stile/gate. Turn L on chalky track which later becomes metalled to
go through woods passing old flint barn to R. Go through gates
and ahead to pass cottages and Victor Morecroft memorial tablet
on flint wall to R at Gumber Farm. Go through gate and along
field edge.

Turn R to go through gate in field corner and follow line of
Stane Street Roman road *(2)*. Follow path along field edge with
the agger of the road in the wooded strip to R. Pass stile on R and
cross line of road to continue up track. It is possible to walk on the
raised road although the path can be overgrown in summer. To
do so look for footpath sign on L soon after stile and follow path
parallel to track. Cross stile and turn R then L to rejoin track.

Continue straight ahead up track to reach car-park from
where the Weald can be glimpsed through the trees ahead.

1 Downland Farming
Here on the dip slope of the South Downs, large arable fields

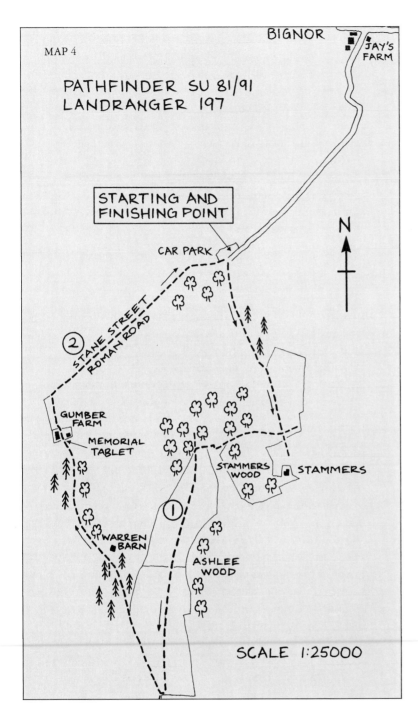

MAP 4

PATHFINDER SU 81/91
LANDRANGER 197

BIGNOR

JAY'S FARM

STARTING AND
FINISHING POINT

CAR PARK

N

STANE STREET
ROMAN ROAD

②

GUMBER
FARM

MEMORIAL
TABLET

STAMMERS
WOOD

STAMMERS

①

WARREN
BARN

ASHLEE
WOOD

SCALE 1:25000

can be seen. Over the centuries, the lower slopes of the Downs have been ploughed and, from time to time, areas of thin soil on the upper slopes have been used to grow crops. Traditionally, though, the Downs were used for sheep pasture. The sheep would graze on the hills during the day and be taken down to the valleys overnight where they would fertilize the

The top of Bignor Hill.

Opposite: View from Bignor Hill.

fields. Centuries of sheep grazing produced a springy, down-land turf rich in plant and animal life which used to be so characteristic of the Downs. Shepherding was both skilful and labour intensive and this way of life has now virtually disappeared with the extensive ploughing of the Downs. This was made possible by a combination of the tractor drawn plough, artificial fertilizers and modern varieties of cereals. Without fertilizers the crops would struggle to survive on the thin soil, some of which is inevitably washed away following successive ploughing. By 1966, only 3.8 per cent of the English chalk supported traditional chalk grassland. Patches of flowers near the top of the Downs and alongside the tracks give some impression of the rich variety of plants that can grow on the Downs.

2 Stane Street

The Roman Stane Street ran from the east gate of Noviomagus, modern Chichester, to London Bridge. Roman methods of road construction were not surpassed until the modern era and the routes were set out with great skill keeping as straight a line as practicable. Stane Street was a major highway and its construction is typical of such roads. In places, the causeway, or agger, which was metalled and cambered, is the standard 22 Roman feet wide with a verge on either side flanked by ditches. However, where it runs along an embankment as it climbs to the crest of the Downs, to the left of the track, the remains of the agger are only a few feet wide and the reason for this has puzzled many archaeologists.

From the top of the hill, the road descends the steep northern escarpment by means of a terraceway and passes close to Bignor Roman Villa. This was a large and prosperous farmstead whose sheep would have grazed the downland turf. It is open to the public and some of the finest mosaics to be found in Britain can be seen there including a bust of Venus surrounded by cupids and Zeus disguised as an eagle carrying off Ganymede to be his cup bearer.

1·5

BOX HILL AND JUNIPER TOP

STARTING AND FINISHING
POINT
Box Hill car-park, opposite the
Information Centre. Signed from
the A24, 5 miles (8 km) north of
Dorking. Pass Burford Bridge
Hotel on R and turn R up zig zag
road. Car-park free to NT
members (TQ 05/15–178513).
LENGTH
4 miles (6.5 km)
ASCENT
450 ft (140 m)

Both the crest and the dip slope of the North Downs are explored on this short walk. It starts and finishes at Box Hill – Surrey's best-known beauty spot and famous picnic site. This classic viewpoint reveals not only a magnificent prospect of the Weald and the South Downs but also the curving ridges of the North Downs.

ROUTE DESCRIPTION (Map 5)

From car-park opposite the Information Centre turn L along road and bear R on parallel path to viewpoint *(1)*. Turn R on NDW and continue along the crest of the Downs into woodland, ignoring the NDW which goes downhill. Pass a grave stone *(2)* and keep ahead down the broad chalk slope *(3)* with a red tiled building *(4)* below on the R. Turn R along road towards Mickleham and at steps on L turn R up access drive. At Little Pinehurst keep ahead on track and in 450 yards (410 m), where track swings R uphill, continue ahead and then go steeply downhill to Juniper Bottom *(5)*. Turn L on track and at NT donation box turn R through gate to follow the slope up to Juniper Top *(5)*. Keep ahead towards woodland and bear L to cross stile beside ornate bench and follow the path through woodland. Here in Ashurst Rough trees such as Scots pine and larch planted earlier this century thrive on the intractable clay-with-flints overlying the chalk.

Ignore first track on R and turn R on cross-track. Where track swings R, keep ahead on grass track to road. Turn L along road and turn R through car-park beside Smugglers Inn. Turn R again onto track and in 25 yards (23 m) bear R up and along cross-path, NDW waymarked with white acorns. Keep ahead to reach the viewpoint on Box Hill and bear R back to car-park.

1 Box Hill
   Box Hill is delightful with a magnificent panorama suddenly bursting into view. The long ridge of the North Downs trails away into Kent which lies to the east. Ahead the vast stretches

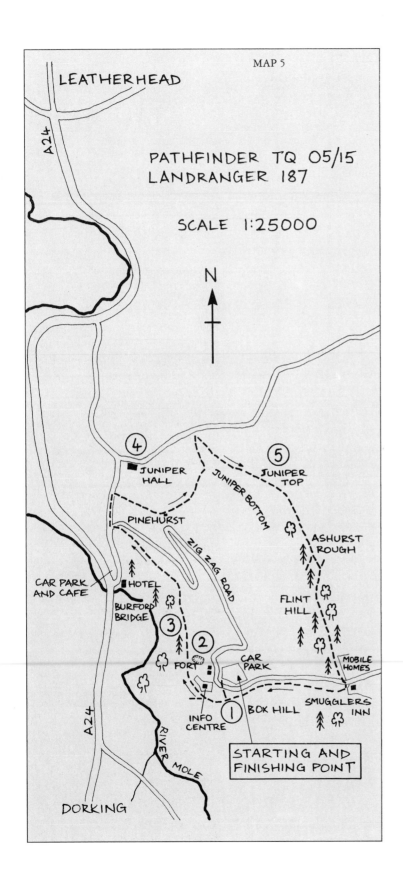

MAP 5

PATHFINDER TQ 05/15
LANDRANGER 187

SCALE 1:25000

N

LEATHERHEAD

A24

④ JUNIPER HALL

JUNIPER BOTTOM

⑤ JUNIPER TOP

PINEHURST

ZIG ZAG ROAD

ASHURST ROUGH

CAR PARK AND CAFE

HOTEL

BURFORD BRIDGE

FLINT HILL

③

② FORT

CAR PARK

MOBILE HOMES

INFO CENTRE

① BOX HILL

SMUGGLERS INN

A24

RIVER MOLE

STARTING AND FINISHING POINT

DORKING

of the Weald reveal extensive woodlands. The South Downs rise in the background with Chanctonbury Ring prominent on the skyline. Immediately below, Dorking sits in the gap carved out by the River Mole. The Roman road Stane Street ran through this gap as does the railway and the A24. Behind Dorking, the Lower Greensand hills rise culminating in Leith Hill whose tower is clearly seen against the skyline. Westwards from the narrow vale of Holmsdale the spire of St Barnabus Church on Ranmore Common marks the continuation of the North Downs.

Box Hill at 680 feet (207 m) dominates the landscape and takes its name from the many groves of evergreen box, whose distinctive, small, glossy leaves are arranged in pairs. It grows naturally in only a few other places in Great Britain. The view-point memorial commemorates the gift of the first 230 acres (93 ha) at Box Hill given to the NT by Saloman Leopold in 1914. He lived nearby at Norbury Park.

Box Hill has hosted many picnics but perhaps the most famous was Jane Austen's Emma's with her party arriving by carriage. Today, many visitors come by car or coach and in the care of the NT, sensitive repairs help to combat the impact of numerous feet and horses' hooves.

2 Gravestone of Peter Labelliere

The gravestone of Peter Labelliere, a major in the Marines who died in July 1800, aged 80, is passed on this route. He was an eccentric resident of Dorking who, it is said, was buried in this spot head down because he believed that as the world was topsy-turvy he might come out right at last.

3 River Cliffs

On the left, the chalk slope drops steeply down to the River Mole below. This spectacular river cliff was carved through the Downs at the end of the last Ice Age and the Mole flows north to join the Thames. The cliff is densely covered with yew and box and is unlikely ever to have been grazed.

4 Juniper Hall

Juniper Hall is hidden in the trees to the right of the red-tiled building. It was once owned by Thomas Broadwood, the piano maker, and is now a Field Study Centre. In 1792, it gave shelter to a group of French aristocrats who had fled to England to escape the worst excesses of the French revolution. It was here that the novelist Fanny Burney, (1752–1840), who was visiting her sister, first met D'Abelière whom she eventually married at Mickleham church in 1793.

View to Mickleham Downs.

The Whites and yew woods, Box Hill.

Almost a hundred years later, in 1890, a fort was built as part of a defence plan for London when there were fears of an invasion by the French. It stands behind the Information Centre on Box Hill.

5 *Juniper Bottom and Juniper Top*

The dry valley of Juniper Bottom and the broad grassy slope leading up to Juniper Top are characteristic features of the dip slope of the Downs and were created towards the end of the last Ice Age when an abundance of meltwater, unable to percolate through the still frozen chalk, cascaded off the hillside. Juniper, with its needle-like leaves and dark blue berries best known as a flavouring for gin, has given its name to this hill, but it is now very rare on the chalk. From Juniper Top there is a superb view over to Norbury Park house and beyond. The NT have reintroduced sheep grazing on the hill to keep the constant threat of invasion by scrub at bay.

Sussex Ouse and Barcombe Mills

STARTING AND FINISHING
POINT
Public car-park in Barcombe
Cross. From Lewes, follow A275
for 3 miles (5 km) towards
Chailey. North of Cooksbridge
bear R at Rainbow Inn and take
first R to Barcombe Cross
(TQ 41/51–422158).
LENGTH
6 miles (9.5 km)
ASCENT
75 ft (20 m)

This level walk in tranquil countryside beside the River Ouse
explores some of the industries that developed over the centuries
along its course.

Route Description (Map 6)

Turn L out of car-park in Barcombe Cross *(1)* and thèn L again
along lane beside Royal Oak public house. Cross estate road to
bear R on narrow, enclosed path and ahead along edge of field. At
angle of fence, turn R over stile and then L parallel to overhead
cables. At second pole, bear R under cables down to path over disused railway *(2)*. Go half L over field and then half R to road. Turn
L along road and after crossing disused railway, turn R and keep
ahead along field edge over stiles to road. This path is thought to
have been part of the Sussex Greensand Way, a Roman road
which linked the London–Lewes Way to Stane Street.

Turn R to pass Barcombe Mills Old Station *(3)*. Just before
road swings R, keep ahead on tarmac path alongside cottages and
then along lane. In front of Barcombe House turn R with track
over weir with toll house on R *(4)*. Cross hump-back bridge and
turn L along river. Turn L over footbridge and along river on L.
Cross stile, turn L over farm bridge and then R along tarmac path.
Before white house turn L to go around back of house *(5)* and
alongside river to Anchor Inn. Go over wide bridge and then turn
L along river and under the disused Lewes to Uckfield railway.

Keep ahead over stiles and with Isfield in the distance turn L
over bridge and R along or near river *(6)*. At T-junction with stile
ahead turn L along track which eventually becomes a lane, ignoring all turnings off. Keep ahead down road passing hornbeams
growing in the woodland strip *(7)*.

At T-junction turn R over stile and across field with farm
buildings on L. Bear R down to footbridge and go ahead with
hedge on R and along enclosed path. At road, turn L and turn R up
farm track to Knowlands Farm. Keep ahead through farmyard

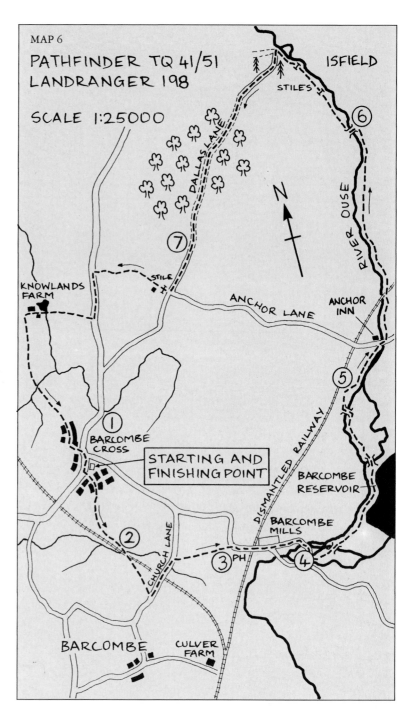

and turn L over stile. Bear R down to R-hand corner of field and follow L-field edge ahead over bridge. Keep ahead to road passing school on R and at T-junction turn R back to Barcombe Cross.

1 Barcombe and Barcombe Cross

Barcombe has several centres and this can lead to some con-

Fishing at Barcombe Mills.

fusion. The modern Barcombe Cross with its tile-hung houses and shops grew up in the late fourteenth century after the Black Death decimated the heart of Barcombe which lies a mile to the south, and the survivors moved to Barcombe Cross. The church, a farm house and a few cottages still remain at Barcombe and since the village sign for Barcombe Cross reads Barcombe, visitors to the area can be misled.

The River Ouse rises as a myriad of fast-flowing streams and brooks upon the High Weald. The river adds enormously to the charm of the flat plain around Barcombe as it makes its leisurely progress through tranquil countryside down to Lewes and then to the sea at Newhaven. Throughout the centuries the river was a major highway transporting people and goods across the Weald. Since Saxon times it has turned many water-wheels, providing power for grinding corn and the manufacture of paper and linseed oil. The river was canalized from Lewes to beyond Lindfield, but the coming of the railways led to its demise as a commercial waterway. Nowadays the canal, railways and mills are disused but the river continues to provide both excellent boating and fishing with fish ladders constructed through the old locks.

2 *Culver Junction to East Grinstead Railway*
In 1882, a new branch line, which became known as the Blue-bell Line because of the carpets of flowers growing on the banks, was built from near Culver Farm to East Grinstead linking into the older Lewes to Uckfield line. Although both are now disused, a small section of this branch line between Horsted Keynes and Sheffield Park has been reopened as a private venture called the Bluebell Railway.

3 *Barcombe Mills Old Station*
It was inevitable that the canal declined, unable to compete with the faster railways. The Lewes to Uckfield line had opened in 1858, branching from the main London line south of Barcombe, and running along the west bank of the river. Barcombe Mills had its own station and sidings which served the mills but the station has now been refurbished as a restaraunt.

4 *Barcombe Mills*
During the first and second centuries AD, the river was forded at Barcombe Mills by the Roman road that ran between London and Lewes. The Domesday Survey of 1086, commissioned by William the Conqueror, records $3\frac{1}{2}$ mills at Barcombe. The apparently elusive half mill referred to in 1086 straddled a border and is also recorded in the neighbouring parish of Isfield.

The Sussex Ouse.

Barcombe Mills mill stones, near the Anchor Inn.

Later records show remarkable continuity of corn, fulling, linseed oil and paper mills. The last of the group of mills at Barcombe, built in 1870, manufactured buttons and was destroyed by fire in 1939. A toll house sits adjacent to the mill bridge and is considered to be the earliest site where tolls were levied in Sussex. When the river was canalized a cut was made around the mill and the humpback Pike's bridge was built over the canal as a crossing point for horses. Goods from the mills were transported by barge and two locks at either side of Pikes bridge provided the necessary step up.

5 *Linseed Oil Mills and Anchor Inn*

From Barcombe Mills the towpath continued further upstream along the east side of the navigation before crossing banks to a group of linseed oil mills. Several millstones remain from the days when linseed oil was mixed with molasses and compressed into cattle feed. The Anchor Inn was built in 1790 as a resting point for the bargees and further upstream the disused Lewes to Uckfield line crosses the river.

6 *Abandoned Meander*

The Parish boundary here loops away to the right on the east side of the river through marshy ground, which was the old course of the river. It may naturally have taken its present course, abandoning its meander but the cut was deepened as part of the navigation.

7 *Hornbeam*

Hornbeam is a characteristic tree of the Low Weald. It thrives on the alluvial soil here and on the intractable Wealden clay where many old hornbeam coppices can be found.

NEWLANDS CORNER AND ST MARTHA'S HILL

STARTING AND FINISHING POINT
Newlands Corner car-park off the A25 to the east of Guildford (TQ 04/14–044492).

LENGTH
5 ¹/₂ miles (9 km). Can be split into two circuits each of approximately 2 ³/₄ miles (4.5 km) by walking along the road from A to B. There is a car-park south of A.

ASCENT
600 ft (180 m)

This short walk visits two of Surrey's best known beauty spots and the site of Chilworth gunpowder works in the Tillingbourne valley. Newlands Corner is on the Chalk ridge of the North Downs while St Martha's church crowns a sandy hilltop. From both there are spectacular views. The valley separating them, formed where the Chalk meets the underlying Gault Clay, has farms dotted along the springline.

ROUTE DESCRIPTION (Map 7)

With your back to Newlands Corner car-park *(1)*, bear R down across grass and turn R on NDW to go alongside edge of trees. Facing downhill from path, St Martha's Hill can be seen half R and there are wide ranging views of the Greensand Hills from the long finger of Blackdown on the R over to the northern slopes of Leith Hill on the L and to the South Downs in the far distance.

Follow path, keeping close to trees on R. In 650 yards (600 m) bear L to pass protruding area of scrub then at end of scrub bear L again downhill and follow path down through trees to road. Cross to go up steps and follow path parallel to road. Leave NDW (A) and turn R on sandy track in front of cottage. Follow to eventually pass through Tyting farmyard and turn L up road.

In 100 yards (90 m) bear L up stepped footpath to pass sandpit on R *(2)*. Ignore path going down valley to L then bear L and follow path ahead. Turn L up wide track, joining NDW, to pass a 1933 Guildford Borough Boundary stone by the fence corner on R and follow track uphill to St Martha's church *(3)*.

Pass to R of church, and leaving NDW, turn R opposite southern gate of churchyard. Pass reservoir fence on R, go over cross-track and steeply downhill on narrow path. Pass Chilworth Manor *(4)* on R and at T-junction turn L along track. Pass two Second World War pill-boxes in the fields and keep ahead. Join the DL to go over the Tillingbourne and then go over the mill stream belonging to the old Chilworth Gunpowder Mills, rem-

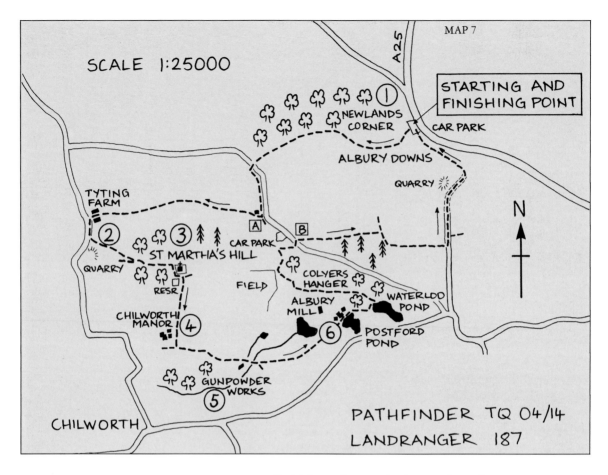

nants of which can be seen in the woods to the R (5).

Shortly after mill stream, leave DL and go ahead over stile and across fields passing the scant foundations of the Admiralty Cordite works built during the First World War. Continue over stile and alongside hedge on R. At Postford Pond turn L to pass Albury mill and trout farm on L (6).

Swing L with track to pass Waterloo Pond. Bear L up path past house on L. Follow through woods past Colyers Hanger on R, old coppice woodland once used to make charcoal for the powder works. At field corner, bear R uphill with path and later bear L to reach sandy cross-track. Turn R down track and at parking area turn L to road (B).

Cross road and turn R along fenced track. Turn R at T-junction then L to go along field edge and follow path to lane. Turn L and follow rough track uphill to pass old chalk quarry on L and later bear L on cross-track to reach Newlands Corner car-park.

1 Newlands Corner

This very popular Open Space with Chalk downland and woodland is managed by the County Council. From Farnham,

Yew woods at Newlands Corner.

the NDW first meets the chalk at Newlands Corner and then follows the escarpment to Dover. The western extremity of the North Downs is a narrow, steep-sided ridge, the Hogs Back, which carries the A31.

2   *St Martha's Hill sandpit*

St Martha's Hill is formed from the Folkestone beds, the youngest beds of the Lower Greensand. This is one of several local sandpits from which building sand has been extracted. The soft sand is easily eroded as can be seen in the split-level path leading up the hill. It is only the hard bands of ironstone (or carstone as it is known locally), which have prevented a far more rapid erosion of the hillside.

3   *St Martha's Hill*

St Martha's Hill is also managed by the County Council and various erosion control measures have been carried out. These include the revetting of the path, which the walk follows up to the church, and the exclusion of the public from some areas to allow heather to regenerate. The effects of the 1987 October storm can clearly be seen on the once heavily-wooded southern slopes.

St Martha's church.

Although it is known that there has been a church on this hilltop since at least the late twelfth century, and possibly earlier, the reason for building it on this isolated site is obscure. By the beginning of the nineteenth century, neglect and the effect of explosions from the Chilworth gunpowder works in the valley below, had left the medieval church in ruins. It was rebuilt and remodelled in 1849 when the tower was removed from the west end and a new central tower built. Copies of prints showing the ruined church can be seen in the chancel. Despite many romantic stories to the contrary, there is no historical evidence that the church was on a main medieval pilgrim route to St Thomas Becket's shrine in Canterbury. Indeed, in Surrey, the 'Pilgrims Way' is a Victorian invention and made its first appearance on early Ordnance Survey maps. There were, of course, early trackways on the Downs but the main Pilgrim route was from London to Canterbury.

A memorial tablet to Yvonne Arnaud (1890–1958), actress and musician after whom Guildford's theatre is named, can be seen just inside the east gate of the churchyard.

4   *Chilworth Manor*

The house is a complex building. The southern wing dates from the seventeenth century and Sarah Churchill, the first Duchess of Marlborough, owned and extended the house between 1721 and 1744.

5   *Chilworth Gunpowder Mills*

From 1625, when the East India company built the first water-

View towards Albury and the Greensand Ridge.

powered mills, until the end of the First World War, gunpow-der was manufactured in this peaceful valley. The ruins of various ages are scattered for over 2 miles (3.2 km) along the Tillingbourne. Guildford Borough Council own the central section of the works which can be visited by turning R off the route to follow the path alongside the mill stream. A short dis-tance along the substantial remains of steam-driven incor-porating mills, erected when the works were modernized in 1885, can be seen. Here saltpetre, sulphur and charcoal were mixed to produce millcake which was then forced through sieves to produce the powder. Much further along the path several groups of vertical millstones and fragmentary remains of the earlier water-driven mills can be found.

6 *Postford and Waterloo Ponds*

These were two of the mill ponds serving a series of gunpow-der and paper mills built in this valley during the eighteenth and nineteenth centuries. Newlands Corner is named after Abraham Newland, a signatory on bank notes, and in 1820 William Cobbett blamed the village for 'two of the most dam-nable inventions that ever sprang from the minds of man under the influence of the Devil' – namely the making of gunpowder and banknotes. This was despite the fact that it was only the paper and not the notes which was produced here.

HYTHE TO DYMCHURCH

STARTING POINT
Hythe station (TR 13 /
23–153347) off the A261, the
northern terminus of the Romney
Hythe and Dymchurch Light
Railway. Parking along Military
Road opposite Green Lane.
FINISHING POINT
Dymchurch Station
(01/02–098292)
PUBLIC TRANSPORT
This linear walk is based on the
Romney Hythe and Dymchurch
Light Railway which runs a regular
service between Easter and
October and some winter specials.
For a timetable write to New
Romney station, Kent, TN28 8PL,
Telephone New Romney (0679)
62353. East Kent buses
(Telephone Chanet [0843]
581333) run a frequent bus service
between Hythe and Dymchurch.
LENGTH
9 miles (14 km)
ASCENT
300 ft (90 m)

From the ancient Cinque Port of Hythe, the walk follows the Royal Military Canal along the edge of Romney Marsh before ascending an ancient cliff face to visit Lympne. The fertile agricultural land of the Marsh is then crossed to reach the busy resort of Dymchurch.

ROUTE DESCRIPTION (Maps 8, 9)

From entrance to Hythe station (1) turn L to cross road bridge over the Royal Military Canal (2) and turn L along Green Lane. Soon bear L up grassy bank to pass SSW stone and go alongside the canal on L. The ancient cliff line can be seen across the fields to the R (3). Pass bridge on L and continue along bank.

Eventually cross road and keep ahead following the path nearest to the canal. Pass a causeway across the canal and sluice gates controlling the entry of water from cutting on L. Continue for a further 300 yards (275 m) then look for, and turn R onto, path to go over footbridge at field corner. Follow fence on R uphill. To the R are the ruins of the Roman fort of Lemanis (4) and Lympne castle and church can be seen on the hilltop.

Turn R with fence then bear L uphill on path with handrail from where there is a good view across the Marsh to Dymchurch. To visit Lympne castle and church (5) turn R at T-junction and later turn R along road. Return to route.

Turn L at T-junction. Cross lane and continue along path. Immediately before road turn L along lane to pass Port Lympne Wildlife Sanctuary on R. Continue on track, then path, going L then R down the ancient cliff line. Turn R along canal bank.

At track, turn L over bridge and along lane. At T-junction turn L then turn R at gates to go along field edge alongside sewer on R. Go to L of large barn and keep ahead along lane to Burmarsh (6).

Turn L at T-junction. Turn R along The Green then L on tarmac path. Cross footbridge and bear R across field going to R of old pillbox to cross footbridge and turn R along fence. Turn L over footbridge and go ahead over field to L of overhead cables. Cross footbridge, go ahead over field to gate then follow sewer on L.

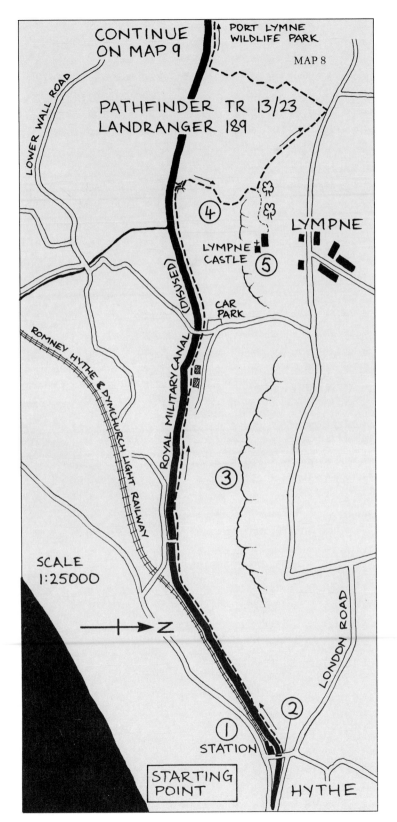

CONTINUE ON MAP 9

PORT LYMNE WILDLIFE PARK

MAP 8

PATHFINDER TR 13/23
LANDRANGER 189

LOWER WALL ROAD

④

LYMPNE

LYMPNE CASTLE

⑤

CAR PARK

ROMNEY HYTHE & DYMCHURCH LIGHT RAILWAY

ROYAL MILITARY CANAL (DISUSED)

③

SCALE 1:25000

→ N

LONDON ROAD

②

①
STATION

STARTING POINT

HYTHE

Stutfall Castle.

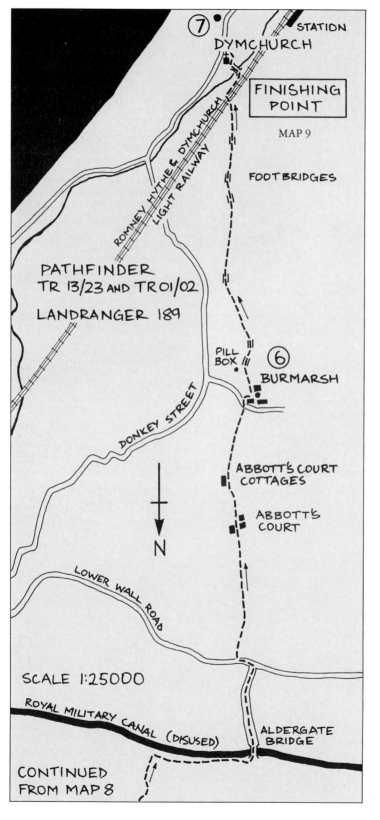

The sea front at Dymchurch.

Turn L over footbridge and go half R across field to footbridge to L of concrete bridge. Go ahead across field, keeping well to R of pond to bridge and stile. Bear L over field to stile and go ahead to cross light railway via footbridge and stiles. Bear R across corner of field to turn R through gate and across field. Turn L over bridge to go down school drive and past church.

Turn R along road to go through Dymchurch. Pass Martello tower number 24 on L *(7)* then turn R on Mill Road and follow signs to Dymchurch station.

1 *Hythe Station*
   Hythe station is the terminus of the Romney Hythe and Dymchurch Light Railway which runs for 13½ miles (22 km) across Romney Marsh to Dungeness. With its 15-inch (381 mm) gauge and one-third scale engines it is the world's smallest public railway and still caters for local needs by running a school train. It was built by Captain Jack Howey, an English millionaire, and opened in 1927. During the Second World War, it transported troops and freight to Dungeness.

2 *Royal Military Canal*
   The plaque on the bridge over the Royal Military Canal records that it extends for 25 miles (40 km) across Romney Marsh to Winchelsea and was constructed in 1805 as defence against the expected invasion of the French under Napoleon. Martello Towers and the flooding of the Marsh were part of the overall plan for the defence of this often threatened shore. The idea that the canal could effectively prevent the advance of the French was a controversial one which fortunately never had to be put to the test.

3 *Lympne hills and Romney Marsh*
   The Greensand cliffs of an ancient shoreline rise steeply from the flat land of Romney Marsh. Waves once lapped around the foot of the Lympne hills but by Roman times the sea had retreated and the Marsh was emerging behind two natural shingle banks. This, combined with the silting-up of estuaries and cutting of drainage channels or sewers, led to much of the northern half of the Marsh being reclaimed or 'inned' by the end of the Roman era.

   The history of this area has been intimately linked with the changing shoreline. Today the Marsh stretches for 25 miles (40 km) along the coast from Hythe to Rye.

4 *Portus Lemanis*
   The Roman harbour of Portus Lemanis was at the foot of these cliffs on a tidal inlet of the River Limnen. A shingle bank, on which part of Hythe was later built, caused the estuary to silt up and by Saxon times the Limnen had found a new route to

Previous page: The Royal Military Canal, near Hythe.

the sea. During terrible storms in 1287, Romney Marsh was flooded and the River Limnen, the modern Rother, again changed its course to meet the sea at Rye on the south side of the Marsh.

The fragmentary remains of the Roman fort of Lemanis, or Stutfall Castle as it was later called, can be seen to the R. Landslips were a problem, even for the Romans, and over the centuries the walls have twisted and moved over 100 yards (90 m) downhill. Lemanis was one of a chain of forts built along the coast between Norfolk and Hampshire in the third century AD by the usurper Carausius, Commander of the British fleet, who declared himself Emperor. They were later used to protect the shore from marauding Saxons.

5 *Lympne castle*

Lympne castle and church stand on top of the cliff line. The castle, the earliest parts of which date from the thirteenth century, was built as a residence for the Archdeacons of Canterbury and the fortifications were for show rather than defence. This attractive and interesting building was restored at the beginning of the century and is open to the public.

6 *Burmarsh*

Burmarsh, one of the earliest settlements on Romney Marsh, is mentioned in a Saxon charter of 850 AD. Lush grass flourished on the fertile alluvial soil and the medieval weaving trade of the Cranbrook–Goudhurst area depended on the Romney Marsh sheep. The soil still supports sheep pasture and arable farming.

7 *Martello Tower and Dymchurch Wall*

The 74 Martello towers built along the coast at the beginning of the nineteenth century were, like the Royal Military Canal, constructed in response to fears of a Napoleonic invasion. A tower on the Bay of Mortella, Corsica, which had successfully beaten off an attack by two British warships in 1794, heavily influenced this strategy. Number 24 is under the care of English Heritage and opens to the public.

Romney Marsh started to emerge behind a shingle bank – the first Dymchurch wall. The present wall protecting the holiday resort is built of Kentish Ragstone.

2·9

TOY'S HILL AND CHARTWELL

STARTING AND FINISHING POINT
Churchill's statue on the Green in Westerham. Car-park is signed off the A25 in the centre of the town (TQ 45/55–447540).
LENGTH
8½ miles (14 km)
ASCENT
1025 ft (310 m)

This walk explores the picturesque Greensand hills around West-erham and Crockham Hill with stunning views across the Weald which have inspired a remarkable number of famous men and women – including General James Wolfe, Winston Churchill and Octavia Hill.

ROUTE DESCRIPTION (Map 10)

From the green in Westerham *(1)* cross the road to go up steps, along enclosed path and over an unusual stone stile. In field, bear L up to stile and then bear L again, ignoring path on L, to reach field corner. Turn L and keep ahead on path through woodland. Where track swings R, keep ahead up path. Turn L through boundary bank then R along it and turn L at gate on R.

Go L along road and turn R through posts to pass commemorative trees *(2)*. About 20 yards (18 m) after trees, turn R on track. At the end of the beech boundary bank, bear L and keep ahead ignoring all tracks off. Turn L along lane and then turn R down lane past French Street Farm.

Swing L up drive past Highview Cottage and keep ahead up main track, through storm-damaged woodland and across Toy's Hill *(3)*. Pass obelisk recording the gift of Weardale to the NT on L then turn R on track to car-park. Cross car-park to go up steps and follow path downhill. Turn L along track, then bear R downhill on path through barrier.

Turn R along road past Octavia Hill's well on L *(4)* from where there is a fine view across the Weald with a patchwork of woods and fields stretching into the distance. Then, 40 yards (35 m) after lane on R, turn R up fenced track towards Chartwell *(5)*. Pass lake and go ahead through kissing gate with oasts on R. At road, turn R to visit Chartwell. Return to route. Turn L along road and in 70 yards (65 m), where road swings L, turn R through kissing gate and keep ahead. Where road eventually swings R, turn L down stepped path. Follow field margin, go over bridge, then bear L

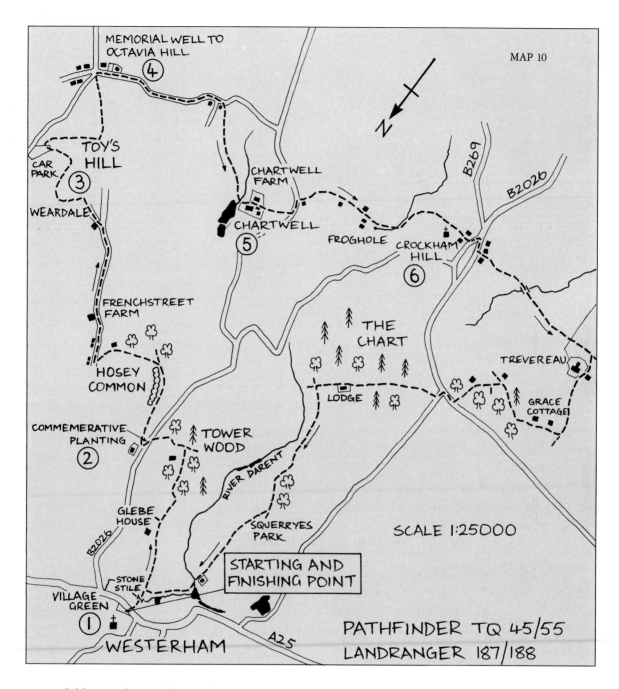

MEMORIAL WELL TO OCTAVIA HILL (4)

MAP 10

N

TOY'S HILL (3)

CAR PARK

WEARDALE

CHARTWELL FARM

CHARTWELL (5)

FROGHOLE

CROCKHAM HILL (6)

B269

B2026

FRENCHSTREET FARM

THE CHART

TREVEREAU

HOSEY COMMON

LODGE

GRACE COTTAGE

COMMEMERATIVE PLANTING (2)

TOWER WOOD

RIVER DARENT

GLEBE HOUSE

B2026

SQUERRYES PARK

SCALE 1:25000

STARTING AND FINISHING POINT

STONE STILE

VILLAGE GREEN (1)

WESTERHAM

A25

PATHFINDER TQ 45/55
LANDRANGER 187/188

across field towards Crockham Hill church *(6)*. Cross stile to pass church on R and keep ahead to road.

At T-junction turn L, then go first R along road. Turn L along Oakdale Lane. At 'Stubblefield' cross stile and go along field edge on R, through woods and along field edge. Go straight across next field to pond, then turn R to stile by cottage. Turn R up metalled track. Pass drive to Grace Cottage and immediately turn R up minor path and along track past cottages. Just before 'Scearn-

bank', bear L up path into woods. At T-junction turn R. Bear L near houses then 25 yards (23 m) later turn L to go steeply up path. Near top, turn R on path and keep ahead along drive.

Turn R along road then turn L on road. Turn R on broad track and follow through woods ignoring all paths off. At lodge, keep ahead on path. Turn L over stile, across field and alongside woods keeping ahead along the Darent valley to join sandy track. Shortly after top of rise, turn R over stile and follow path across fields from where there is a splendid view over Westerham to the North Downs. At lodge turn L on track. Turn R over footbridge opposite pond to go along field edge. Just after tennis court turn L on path to Westerham.

1 *Westerham*

On the green of this attractive town, its association with two famous people is remembered – General James Wolfe and Winston Churchill. Wolfe is commemorated here brandishing a sword aloft. He was born in Westerham on 2 January 1727 and died in battle on the Heights of Abraham in Quebec on 13 September 1759 at the age of only 32. Churchill lived at Chartwell, which can be visited on the walk, from 1924 until shortly before his death in 1965. A powerful bronze statue capturing Churchill in a pensive mood as he sits slumped, in his slippers, is the work of sculptor Oscar Nemon. The parish church of St Mary the Virgin is, like many buildings to be seen on route, built from local sandstone. It contains the Royal Arms of Edward VI, Henry VIII's only son. The Arms are the only ones of this period to have survived within a parish church.

At one end of the town lies Quebec house, Wolfe's childhood home. In the stable block is an exhibition of his famous victory and the house itself contains Wolfe family memorabilia. At the other end of the town lies Squerryes Court, a lovely red-brick manor house dating from the time of William and Mary. There are fine 200-year-old collections of tapestries, furniture and porcelain, and landscaped gardens with lakes which Wolfe often visited. It was within the grounds of Squerryes Court that he received his first commission, at the age of fourteen. Both Quebec House, now owned by the NT, and Squerryes Court are open to the public.

2 *Commemorative Planting at Hosley Common*

Two trees, a lime and an oak, were planted on behalf of Trees for the Future by the Duke and Duchess of Kent on the 23 March 1988 to commemorate the extensive damage caused by

Across the Weald from Toy's Hill.

the 1987 storm. The multi-stemmed beech hedges along the track survive from the days when pollarding kept the young shoots out of the way of browsing cattle.

3 *Toy's Hill*

Toy's Hill was a beautiful mixed woodland of beech and pine trees. The hill rises to a height of over 800 ft (244 m), the highest point in Kent, and consequently it suffered extensive damage in the 1987 storm. Paths have been cleared, but in many areas the fallen trees have been left to encourage wildlife. With minimum intervention from the NT there has been vigorous regeneration. Young trees are thriving in the light.

Originally it was part of the common land of Brasted Chart and the single, pollarded beeches are reminders of the days when animals grazed in the woodland. In 1906, a house called Weardale was built at Toy's Hill, set upon a terrace and surrounded by landscaped grounds. It was demolished in 1939 and now only traces remain of its former glory.

4 *Octavia Hill's well*

Octavia Hill (1838–1912), one of the most influential people of the nineteenth century, sank this well near the cottages to the south of Toy's Hill for the benefit of local people. One of her sisters lived in a house above the cottages and Octavia was a frequent visitor. At a time when women were not encouraged to take part in public life Octavia devoted her time, energy and slender resources to housing reform and the poor laws, asserting the rights of commoners and protecting open spaces and public rights of way. With financial help from John Ruskin she set up some of the earliest housing associations in the slum areas of London. Renowned for her vigour and strength of character, Ruskin's only criticism of her was that she 'wanted to dress anyhow and could rarely be persuaded to buy a new hat'. As one of the three co-founders of the National Trust (see page 172) her vision inspired others and Toy's Hill was given to the Trust shortly after its foundation. It is now one of several open spaces owned by the NT along this Greensand ridge.

5 *Chartwell*

Chartwell is in the ownership of the NT and is open to the public. The house stands in a steep, wooded valley and its name stems from a natural well or spring. Chartwell itself is not a distinguished building but it was its setting and views that Churchill loved. The terrace around the house sweeps down to a series of ponds and lakes that Churchill designed and he spent many hours painting in the gardens.

6 *Crockham Hill and Froghole*

At Froghole the path descends 133 steps through the garden of

Churchill on Westerham Green.

In
LOVING MEMORY
OF MIRANDA HILL
BORN JAN 1 1836 DIED MAY 31 1910
BLESSED ARE THE PURE IN HEART
FOR THEY SHALL SEE GOD
AND
OF HER SISTER
OCTAVIA HILL
1838 · 1912
HARRIOT YORKE
1842 · 1930

Octavia Hill's grave.

a lovely thatched cottage. In 1596 there was a great landslip in this area when the Greensand slipped over the underlying clay changing the local landscape.

Octavia Hill lies, in a simple grave under a yew tree, in Crockham Hill churchyard. She shares it with her sister Miranda and her lifelong friend and helper Harriot Yorke. Octavia spent the last few years of her life living nearby with her friend in the heart of the countryside she loved. A marble effigy of her lies by the altar.

67

2·10

WYE AND CRUNDALE DOWNS

STARTING AND FINISHING
POINT
Free car-park in Wye almost
opposite church. Wye is 4 miles
(6 km) north-east of Ashford,
signed off the A28
(TR 04/14–054468).
LENGTH
8 miles (13 km)
ASCENT
825 ft (250 m)

This scenic Downland walk visits Crundale church, perched high upon the Downs, and Wye and Crundale National Nature Reserve with its spectacular, gash-like valley, the Devil's Kneading Trough.

ROUTE DESCRIPTION (Map 11)

From car-park turn R along road and bear L on path through churchyard (1), joining NDW. Follow to road. Go ahead along Occupation Road and then track. Look for gateway on R and bear L across field towards radio mast, leaving NDW. Cross road and go up to stile to L of mast. Go ahead over road and along path then turn R along field edge to stile. Bear L up to highest point in field and go up through woodland to top of scarp slope. Keep ahead over grassy area from where there is a superb view over the Great Stour Valley to the Downs beyond along which the northern branch of the NDW runs to Canterbury.

Go through gate and at woodland edge bear L across field (path may be indistinct) towards pond on L. Continue ahead down across field, well to L of overhead cables, to stile through woodland strip. Bear L parallel to overhead cables (path may be indistinct) to woodland tip. From wood corner, go under cables and ahead over two fields up towards church. After second field keep ahead up bank to bear L across stile and up to track. Detour L to visit Crundale church (2).

Turn R along track with extensive views ahead and down to dry valleys on each side. Continue through woodland. At T-junction, turn R down track and then L on track. After woods, keep ahead along field edge, through gates, then turn R along fence on R. Turn L along farm drive to road. Go ahead into National Nature Reserve (3), joining NDW. Bear R along woodland edge to stile. Keep ahead and turn R through gate with the Devil's Kneading Trough on L, leaving NDW. Go ahead and down steep, stepped path to road.

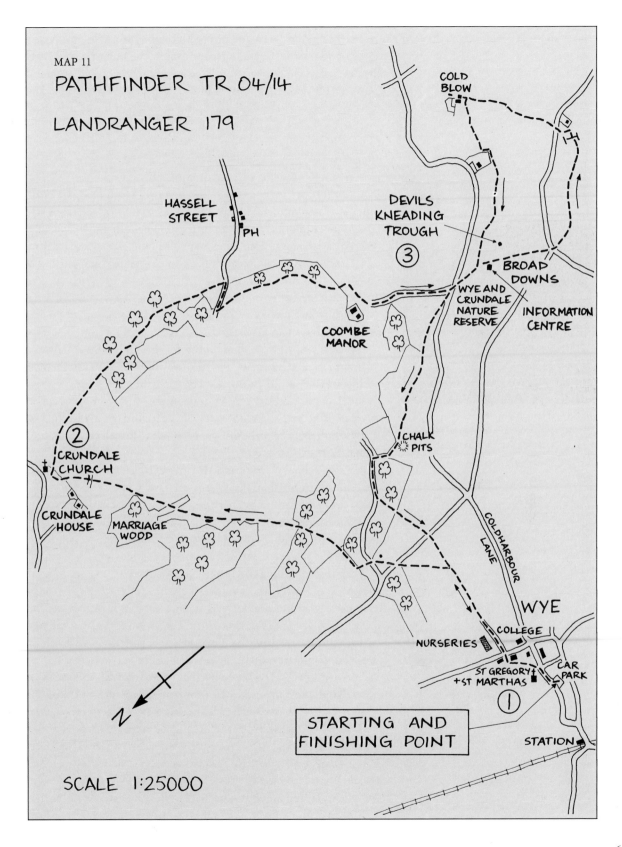

MAP 11
PATHFINDER TR 04/14
LANDRANGER 179

HASSELL STREET
PH

DEVILS KNEADING TROUGH
③

COOMBE MANOR

WYE AND CRUNDALE NATURE RESERVE

COLD BLOW

BROAD DOWNS

INFORMATION CENTRE

②
CRUNDALE CHURCH

CRUNDALE HOUSE

MARRIAGE WOOD

CHALK PITS

COLDHARBOUR LANE

WYE

NURSERIES

COLLEGE

ST GREGORY + ST MARTHAS

CAR PARK

①

N

STARTING AND FINISHING POINT

STATION

SCALE 1:25000

Turn L and at road junction go straight over stile and bear L across field to stile. Cross track and stile to turn L along field edge. Bear R across field with woodland on L to stile and keep ahead across fields and stiles. Before house, turn L over footbridge and stile and cross field to road. Go up track to top of the escarpment. Just before barns, turn L over stile to follow NDW back to Wye. Keep ahead across fields. Follow path around a wire fence and ahead to pass Devil's Kneading Trough. Then retrace steps to road. Go up track, immediately turn L through gate and bear R along fence to follow ridge with a view down to Wye. Pass old chalk pits and at fence corner turn R and then R again over stile down to road. Turn L and look for, and bear L down, path and keep ahead on track between fields. Cross road and continue along track to road. Cross and bear L on path back to church and car-park.

1 Wye and its church

The historic town of Wye grew up on the east bank of the Great Stour. The majestic church of St Gregory and St Martin with its peal of eight bells is the focal point of this attractive town. In the church, beautifully-worked pew covers and kneelers depict in colourful scenes the life and history of the town. In 1935, JLW Sawbridge, Earl of Drax restored and hung a fine collection of his family's hatchments in the church. Hatchments, carried at funerals, displayed the armorial bearings of the dead.

Wye college, part of the Universtiy of London, stands next to the church. The three stooks of corn in its coat of arms, displayed over the main entrance, depicts the specialism of the college, agriculture. Recently it has also become well-known for its graduates in landscape ecology and design.

2 Crundale Church

This delightful church with beautiful flint work stands alone at the top of the hill overlooking its parish. A life-sized figure clad in priest's robes and carved from a marble slab records the death of Reverend John Sprot who was rector at Crundale from 1431 until his death in 1466. At his bequest all the married parishioners were given 40d, and the unmarried 12d.

A painting of Queen Anne's Royal Arms after the union of Scotland and England in 1707, hangs on the west wall of the church. Previously she had borne the Stuart Arms and so these Arms at Crundale are sometimes called Queen Anne's second coat.

3 Wye and Crundale National Nature Reserve and the Devil's Kneading Trough

Wye and Crundale National Nature Reserve is managed by the Nature Conservancy Council who have reintroduced sheep-

The church at Crundale.

The Devil's Kneading Trough.

grazing here and on other reserves to manage chalk grassland in the traditional way. Before sheep can be brought onto the reserve a great deal of hard work needs to be carried out.

Stock-proof fences, and stiles to maintain public access, need to be built, but the hardest work is removing all the scrub and ensuring that no poisonous yew remains. Burning the scrub would be counter-productive as the resulting potash would enrich the soil changing the nature of the grassland.

The Devil's Kneading Trough is a spectacular, deep, dry valley. The name of Devil is often associated with natural or man-made features that appear to have no logical explanation. Its origin, however, can be traced back to the last Ice Age when the Downs and Weald lay near to the ice sheets that covered the rest of Britain and was very like the Arctic tundra of today. Reindeer roamed the lowlands feeding on the sparse vegetation. The ground was permanently frozen except for a surface layer that thawed out during the day and froze at night. Repeated freeze-thaw action caused the chalk to shatter and this debris was carried downhill by torrents of meltwater unable to percolate through the frozen subsoil. As the climate warmed up over a period of about 500 years the Devil's Kneading Trough was gradually formed. Small fragments of chalk within a chalky mud, known as Coombe deposits, slipped down from the higher slopes onto the valley floor.

2·11

CRANBROOK AND GOUDHURST

STARTING AND FINISHING
POINT
Cranbrook town centre signed off
the A229. Car-park is near the
junction of Stone Street and The
Hill (TQ 63/73–777359).
LENGTH
10 miles (16 km)
ASCENT
400 ft (120 m)

From Cranbrook, with its attractive weatherboarded houses, the walk ascends the Greensand ridge to Goudhurst and passes through hop gardens and past oast houses so typical of this part of Kent.

ROUTE DESCRIPTION (Maps 12–14)

Turn L out of car-park to go up Stone Street in Cranbrook (1). Turn L with road to go along the High Street, passing Lloyds Bank on L, and turn R along New Road opposite. Cross road to go up footpath opposite through woods. In 180 yards (165 m), turn L off main track. At cross-track go R and almost immediately L. Turn L on sandy track, ignore paths off then where track bears L, turn R on wide track. In valley bottom, go ahead up path opposite. At top, bear L along main track passing worked coppice on R.

Cross road and turn L. At end of fence turn R to go along field edge. At field corner, turn L and almost immediately R over ditch and ahead along field edge from where the moated Glassenbury House and grounds can be seen to the R. Keep ahead up drive, past houses on L and along field edge from where Goudhurst church comes into view on the Greensand ridge. Turn L with track, then, just past end of field corner, turn R with track. At field gate ahead go L along field edge on R, through gate and wood and along field edges. At T-junction, turn R on track alongside wood.

Pass through Snugley Farm, an old hop farm where new developments can be expected. Immediately in front of converted barn, where concrete road goes L, turn R across grass between house and shed and ahead down concrete track (2). Continue along and then up track. At road, turn R up lane. Turn L at T-junction then in 22 yards (20 m) turn R up steps and over stile. Cross road to go through churchyard at Goudhurst (3).

Turn R by church tower to go through churchyard and ahead

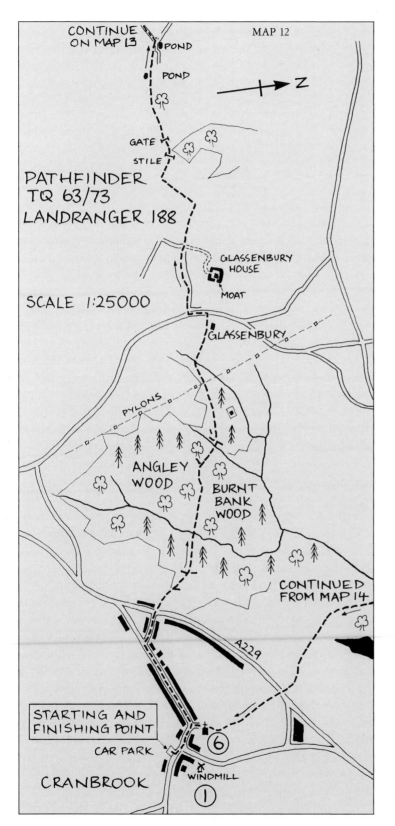

CONTINUE
ON MAP 13

POND

POND

MAP 12

Z

GATE

STILE

PATHFINDER
TQ 63/73
LANDRANGER 188

SCALE 1:25000

GLASSENBURY
HOUSE

MOAT

GLASSENBURY

PYLONS

ANGLEY
WOOD

BURNT
BANK
WOOD

CONTINUED
FROM MAP 14

A229

STARTING AND
FINISHING POINT

CAR PARK

6

CRANBROOK

WINDMILL

1

A hop garden near Bockingfold Farm.

along road. At end house on L, Cloth Edge, turn L on drive past garage, through gate and ahead down field to stile. Turn R on road. Turn L on road to Curtisden Green and bear L on track to Ladham house. At entrance, keep ahead through gate and along R side of tree nursery and hop garden to reach Bockingfold Farm *(4)*.

Bear L under chute between buildings and along track. Where this turns L, bear R through gate and along edge of hop garden. Turn L on first track going past straining wires. At field edge turn R, then, just after field edge turns L, look for and scramble across ditch (footbridge missing). Turn L along track then R along field edge. Turn R through gate and go straight across field to cross stile in far R corner. Go ahead through wood and alongside hop garden. At road turn L, then immediately R and R again up track. Shortly before oast house, bear L and follow track to go along L sides of fields and through woodland strip. At wood edge turn R for 10 yards (9 m) then L to go straight across field to track and ahead alongside fence on L. Go over cross-track and keep ahead along wood and field edges.

Cross road to go along field edge opposite. Turn L along lane then R over stile and along R side of field. At field corner, go ahead through wood, parallel to field on R. At wood corner bear R down across field to cross causeway between lakes. Go up path starting from R side of causeway, over stile and ahead up L side of field. Go through gate, across field to R-hand gate and along field edge.

Cross lane to Hazelden farm and oasts on L to go over stile opposite, to L of cottage. Follow field edge alongside trees on R. At wood corner go ahead parallel to hedge on R. 35 yards (30 m) before field corner turn R through double gates and alongside hedge on R. Turn L on road. Turn R along A262 to Goudhurst, with extreme care, passing 'The House that Jack Built'. Turn L down private road to Kennel Holt Hotel. When this swings R, go ahead down track to cross stream and go up through woods. Keep ahead up through coppiced chestnut *(5)*. Go through barrier (stile) at field corner and keep ahead. Cross stile and later go through old kissing gate. Bear L through trees then L again to follow path alongside fence on R. Continue along drive and cross road to go along path between houses. Go through gate and ahead up field. Turn R through gate in top corner of field and follow path round school. At end, turn L to go through gate and follow enclosed path to reach churchyard. Bear R through churchyard passing church on L *(6)* and continue ahead down Stone Street to reach car-park.

1 Cranbrook

This attractive town is dominated by the Union Mill, a work-

The Union mill at Cranbrook.

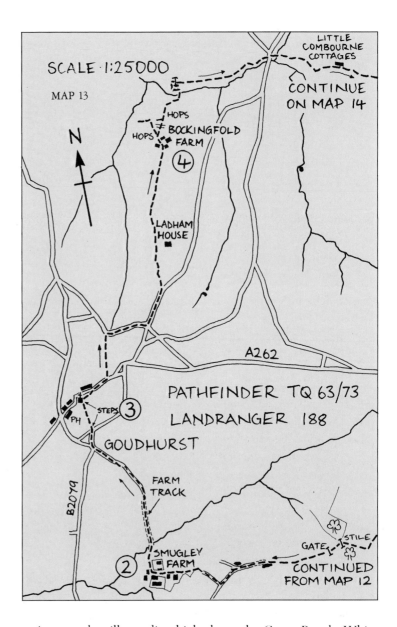

ing smock mill standing high above the Crane Brook. White weatherboarded and tile-hung buildings so typical of this part of Kent immediately catch the eye. In 1331, Edward III granted passports to Flemish weavers in order to encourage the home production of high-quality cloth. Many settled in Cranbrook with its plentiful supply of soft water from the local springs and proximity to Romney Marsh with its large flocks of sheep. The town grew prosperous and the fine, timber-framed buildings along the old streets reflect this. The clothiers built cloth halls which were part residences and part storage space. Lloyds Bank, although almost totally rebuilt, gives some impression of what a medieval cloth hall would have looked like.

Most of the cloth was exported to Flanders to be dyed and finished.

2 *Hops and hop pickers*

Ale brewed from malt without the addition of hops, was the drink of medieval England but both beer and hops were imported by Tudor times. The traditional date given for the planting of the first hop garden in England is 1520 at Westbere, near Canterbury. In Kent, common land was enclosed early on, making more land available for hops on the lighter, sandy soils. The Wealden woodlands provided an ample supply of coppice wood for hop poles and fuel for drying the hops. Before mechanization, hop picking was very labour intensive and migrant workers supplemented the local labour force. With the advent of the railways, hundreds of Londoners descended on Kent for the picking season. Working conditions were extremely primitive and charitable and missionary organizations campaigned for hopper houses to be built to shelter the families. After the Second World War, machines gradually replaced the pickers.

3 *Goudhurst*

Goudhurst sits in a commanding position on the Greensand ridge with St Mary's church overlooking the Weald. The sandstone church dates from the thirteenth century but was heavily restored in Victorian times and its chief glories are the Colepeper family monuments. Like Cranbrook, Goudhurst was a centre for the medieval weaving industry.

4 *Hop gardens*

Although the amount of land planted with hops has fallen during this century, Kent still produces more hops than any other county. Methods of stringing the hops have changed over the years and the modern geometric wirework seen in the gardens demands skilled labour. New wilt-resistant varieties of hop are grown in the Wealden area to combat the disease that once threatened the prosperity of the industry. The hops are dried in oasts and the design of these has varied. The round oast was introduced at the beginning of the last century only to be replaced by square ones a hundred years later. All sport a distinctive cowl pivoted so that the hot air outlet will always be turned away from the wind to increase the draught. Every hop farm had at least one oast and many disused ones have been converted into houses.

5 *Chestnut coppicing*

Sweet chestnut was planted in the Wealden woods to provide a regular supply of hop poles. Today it is coppiced for poles and fencing, the stems being cleft into four to produce the characteristic palings.

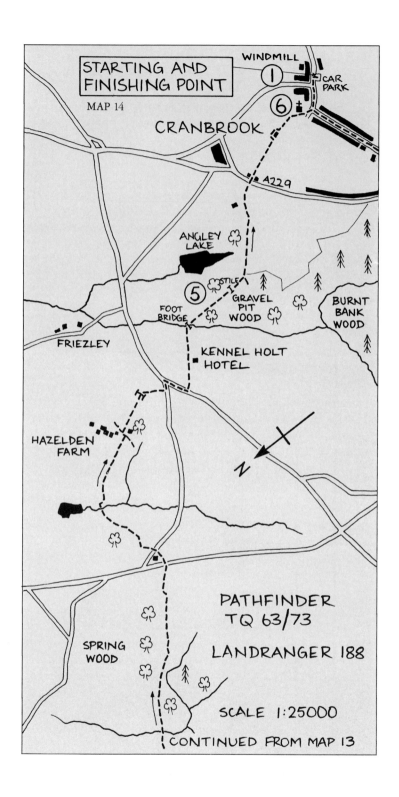

A weatherboarded oast house.

6 *St Dunstan's, Cranbrook*

'The Cathedral of the Weald' took two centuries to complete. This spacious church dating from the mid-fourteenth century and built with local sandstone reflects the prosperity of the medieval town. It replaced a much humbler building. The church clock has an original gravity escapement invented by Lord Grimthorp and the works were a prototype for 'Big Ben'.

HASTINGS TO WINCHELSEA

STARTING POINT

Hastings East Cliff car-park signed off the A259 where it turns westward along the sea front (TQ 81/91−826094).

FINISHING POINT

Winchelsea bus stop outside St Thomas's Church (TQ 81/91 − 904174).

PUBLIC TRANSPORT

The Hastings & District Bus Company, telephone Hastings (0424) 433711, operate a regular service between the two towns. The Marsh Link local train service can also be used, telephone Hastings (0424) 429325.

LENGTH

9 miles (14 km)

ASCENT

725 ft (220 m)

A scenic walk between two Cinque Ports, from the bustling resort of Hastings to the quiet refinement of Winchelsea with the sandstone cliffs near Hastings contrasting with the flat reclaimed land of the levels.

ROUTE DESCRIPTION (Maps 15−17)

Go up Tamarisk steps alongside the Dolphin Inn opposite the net sheds at the foot of East Cliff *(1)*. At top of steps turn L along road, then R up steps. At top, turn R past entrance to cliff railway and up more steps to reach Hastings Country Park. Looking back there is a good view to the ruins of Hastings Castle *(2)* on top of West Cliff.

Keep ahead alongside fence on R to pass the Armada beacon *(3)* on L. Follow path when it starts to go downhill. Turn R down steps towards Ecclesbourne Glen. At bottom, keep ahead up stepped path and at top turn L on first grassy path then bear R on path between bushes. This next section of path has been diverted away from the cliff edge because of erosion *(4)*.

Follow path later going downhill. At large waymark post number 6, turn R up rocky path and alongside fence on L, over cross-track and ahead through gate. Turn L downhill with path by 'dangerous cliff' sign to go down steps. At path junction, keep R and ahead uphill alongside fence on R, ignoring R turn down to beach. Just before path goes from bracken into trees, turn R by waymark post up stepped path, along field edge, then down stepped path. Turn L on grassy path signed to Fairlight Road. Cross stile and keep ahead. Just before road, turn R then L through gap to cross road to drive and large footpath sign. Immediately turn R through gate to go down track from where the Weald can be seen stretching out ahead and a view of Pett Levels unfolds to the R.

At track end, pass building on R and keep ahead on narrow path down through woods. Crossing stiles, go ahead to wood

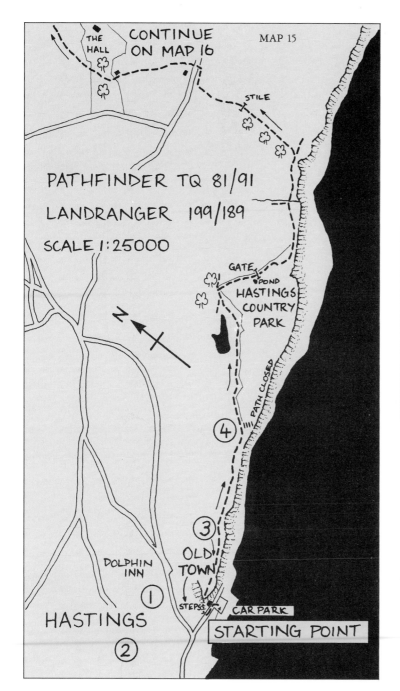

CONTINUE ON MAP 16

THE HALL

MAP 15

STILE

PATHFINDER TQ 81/91

LANDRANGER 199/189

SCALE 1:25000

N

GATE

POND

HASTINGS COUNTRY PARK

PATH CLOSED

④

③

DOLPHIN INN

OLD TOWN

STEPS

CAR PARK

STARTING POINT

HASTINGS

①

②

The start of the walk at Hastings.

edge, straight across field and ahead through woods keeping to R of grassy area. Cross drive and follow path opposite down through woods and ahead across field from where The Hall, a large Victorian building, can be seen to the R. At field edge turn R alongside hedge on L. 40 yards (37 m) before crossing track turn L through hedge and keep ahead, going diagonally across field under overhead cables. At wood edge, keep ahead on path down

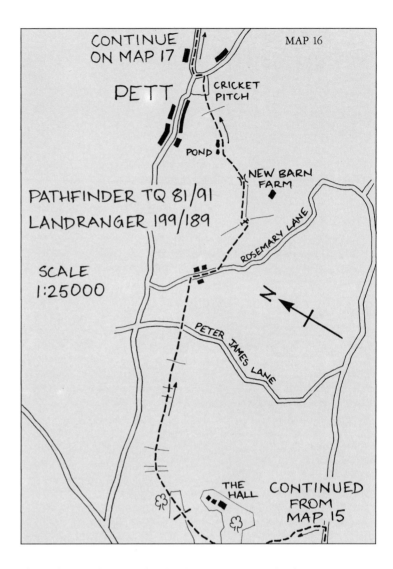

through woods, over footbridges and across field to lane. Keep straight ahead over stiles, across fields, through woodland strip and over fields to lane well to L of oast house. Cross lane and follow field edge to lane.

Turn R to pass Stream Cottage on L then turn L through the second field gate on L and go up field to cross stile. Go straight ahead over brow of hill from where Dungeness with its nuclear power station, comes into view. Cross stile/gate and bear R downhill alongside hedge on R. At field corner, go ahead over footbridge and up alongside hedge on L. Cross stile then bear R in front of second stile. Cross field, passing woodland corner on L, then bear L up to stile. Go ahead across field, then go half R over field and cricket pitch to road.

Turn L, then turn R along Elm Lane. Where lane turns R, go straight ahead over metal barrier and along enclosed track. Cross

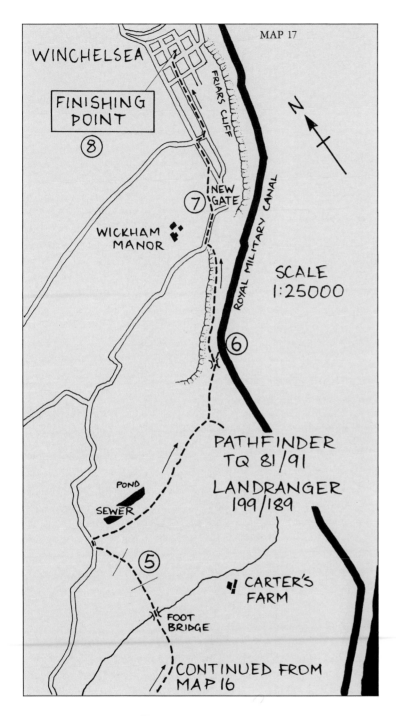

MAP 17

WINCHELSEA

FINISHING POINT

⑧

FRIARS CLIFF

N

NEW GATE

⑦

WICKHAM MANOR

SCALE 1:25000

ROYAL MILITARY CANAL

⑥

PATHFINDER TQ 81/91

LANDRANGER 199/189

POND

SEWER

⑤

CARTER'S FARM

FOOT BRIDGE

CONTINUED FROM MAP 16

footbridge and go straight up field to stile then straight down field to stile in field corner. From the hilltop Pett Levels and Dungeness can again be seen (5). Bear slightly L across field to gate, turn R along lane and immediately before bridge turn R down to metal barrier and go along bank of sewer.

Keep alongside sewer following field edges then grassy track.

Where track turns R keep ahead alongside sewer. Just before sewer meets the Royal Military Canal (6) coming in from R, turn L over footbridge and bear R on path keeping close to ancient cliff face on L. Cross wet area to stile and follow cliff to lane. Turn R then, 45 yards (40 m) before medieval gateway, turn L through gate and follow fence on R parallel to deep town ditch (7). The Tudor Wickham Manor can be glimpsed up to the L. Cross stile and bear R up across field to stile. Turn L on enclosed path. Cross road and turn R along pavement to reach church and bus stop, on R, in centre of Winchelsea (8).

1 *Hastings and the Cinque Ports*

Hastings is the most westerly of the five original Cinque Ports. The origins of this Confederation are lost in antiquity but it certainly dates from Saxon times. Long before the days of the Royal Navy they provided the Sovereign with warships and crew. In return, the ports enjoyed a number of privileges including freedom from Royal taxes and the right to hold their own courts. The portsmen were proud of their independence and many grew rich through smuggling and piracy.

William the Conqueror made Hastings his principal port but gradual silting up of the estuary, accentuated by the terrible gales of 1287, led to the decline of the town and harbour. Its fortunes were revived when the seaside became popular and today it has all the trappings of a typical resort. The old town nestling under the East Cliff and the tall, tarred wooden net shops where the fishing nets are dried are reminders of Hastings before the days of the holiday maker.

2 *Hastings castle*

The ruins can be seen across the town on West Cliff. Nearly half of the castle has long since disappeared over the cliff face as a result of landslips and quarrying. Both the castle and St Clement's Caves below it can be visited.

3 *The Armada Beacon*

Long before the Spanish Armada set sail in 1588, Hastings, like most of the Cinque Ports, had silted up and so had to hire ships from more distant ports to fulfil its obligations. Beacons were lit to warn of the approach of the enemy fleet and in 1988 beacons were again lit on many hilltops throughout the Downs and Weald to celebrate the 400th anniversary of the defeat of the Spaniards.

4 *Coastal erosion*

The rock-strewn shore seen along the coastal path bears wit-

Cliff erosion near Hastings.

The town ditch and gate at Wickham Manor.

ness to past landslips where the sandstone cliffs have fractured and moved across the slippery clay beneath. The cliffs are continually being eroded and fears of future landslips has led to the closure of part of the cliff path.

5 *Pett Levels and Dungeness*

Pett Levels have, like Romney Marsh to the north (see page 60), been 'inned' or reclaimed from the sea by the natural build-up of alluvium behind a shingle bank and the cutting of sewers or dykes to drain this fertile soil. The lakes and reed-lined sewers are a haven for many water birds. The great shingle mass that is Dungeness has gradually evolved over the centuries. Successive bands of shingle have been, and continue to be, deposited by the easterly tidal currents.

6 *Royal Military Canal*

See page 60.

7 *Old Winchelsea and New Gate*

Old Winchelsea and Rye joined the Confederation of Cinque Ports in 1191 as Limbs of Hastings and, as Hastings declined in importance, they became head ports. Old Winchelsea situated on the marshes somewhere to the south-east of Rye was badly affected by storms throughout the thirteenth century. By 1281, much of the town had been claimed by the sea and Edward I commissioned the new town on the hilltop where it now stands some 6 miles (10 km) from the sea. New Gate and the massive town ditch were outer defences cutting off the southerly approach.

8 *Winchelsea*

The streets were laid out on the gridiron principal which can clearly be seen today but Edward I's ambitious plans for the town were never completely fulfilled. The imposing church of St Thomas is nothing more than the chancel and side chapels of what was planned as a magnificent building. Seven major raids by the French over the next two centuries and the gradual silting up of its new harbour led to the decline of the town. There was a revival in Georgian times and it later became a popular haunt for many authors and actors including Edward Lear, Ellen Terry, EF Benson, Henry James and Joseph Conrad. The town is well-worth exploring and the coastal plain can be seen from Strand Gate perched on top of the ancient cliff.

2·13

WEY–ARUN CANAL AND DOWNS LINK

STARTING AND FINISHING POINT
Sydney Wood Forestry Commission car-park, 1½ miles (2.5 km) west of Alfold Crossways on the A281 (TQ 03/13–026352.
LENGTH
11 miles (18 km)
ASCENT
200 ft (60 m)

This interesting walk through woodlands, once a centre of the Wealden glass industry, explores the disused Wey–Arun canal and the old Guildford to Horsham railway. It is particularly recommended in spring when bluebells, primroses and wood anemones carpet the woodland floor.

ROUTE DESCRIPTION (Maps 18–21)

From the car-park entrance, with back to the road, go along tarmac track towards Sedgehurst. Some 30 yards (27 m), after stream, bear R from tarmac track parallel with boundary bank

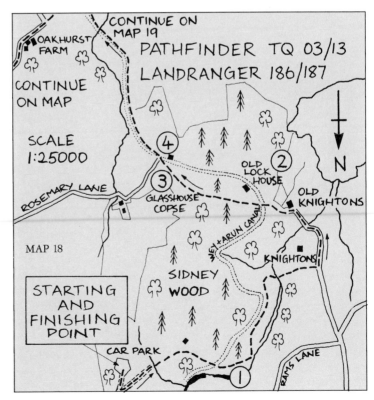

keeping Sedgehurst on the L. Then, 60 yards (55 m) later, after crossing the disused Wey–Arun canal *(1)*, turn L on path which runs alongside the canal for a short distance. Where the canal turns L, go ahead down path over stream and past farm buildings on R. Continue along drive to road. Turn L passing Old Knightons, a Wealden timber-framed house. Keep ahead on track through Sydney Wood which recrosses the canal *(2)*.

Keep ahead through woods *(3)*, over cross-track ignoring all turnings off. At T-junction turn R alongside house to cross canal *(4)*. Turn L beside it. Keep ahead, ignoring paths off. Turn L on cross-track, joining SBP to go over canal and ahead into woods. Follow L-edge of field through gate into farmyard and ahead down track to road. Turn L and then R down Pigbushe Lane, with views back to the Greensand hills on the L. Go through farmyard and at woods bear L on path. Cross stream and immediately bear L on path. Turn L through gate adjacent to boundary bank. Pass pond on L and bear R through gate and ahead to cross-track. Go ahead along middle track.

With school buildings on R go ahead over the drive through gate and bear L over field to left of house. Keep ahead along road and turn L towards Baynards. At T-junction, go ahead on path to left of deer fence. Follow through high kissing gates, over cross-track and along field edge to stile into woodland. There are wide ranging views from Chanctonbury Hill on the South Downs back to Blackdown.

Keep ahead through woodland, joining the DL *(5)* at track on L. Continue ahead, then turn L over stile to Baynards, leaving SBP. Turn L over footbridges and bear R down steps into railway cutting. Keep ahead under road bridge and then turn L and immediately R alongside the refurbished Baynards station, to rejoin and follow the trackbed of the former railway.

About ¼ mile (400 m) after crossing the Cranleigh stream, bear L on crossing path down embankment and over stile, leaving DL. Keep ahead along field edge. At field corner, turn L through ditch and R to follow field edge and go ahead between fields to L of house. Turn R along road and immediately L on track. Turn L along road, to go alongside the canal. At T-junction turn L along road and immediately turn R and then bear R on track. Keep ahead across field to L of mobile homes and follow lane to road *(6)*. Turn L and then R along road to Dunsfold around the aerodrome and back to car-park.

1 Wey–Arun Canal

On 29 September 1816 the Wey–Arun canal, which had been built by local contractors, was opened for traffic. For the first time, London and the River Thames were linked to the south coast and the English Channel. An attempt had been made in

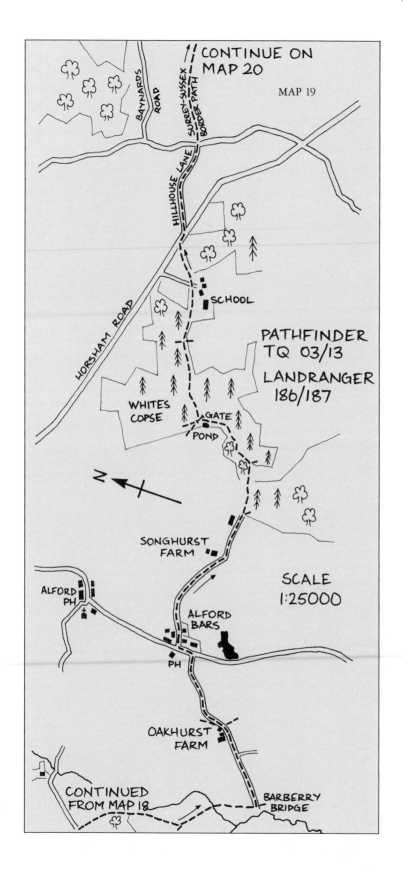

CONTINUE ON MAP 20

MAP 19

BAYNARDS ROAD

SURREY-SUSSEX BORDER PATH

HILLHOUSE LANE

SCHOOL

HORSHAM ROAD

PATHFINDER TQ 03/13

LANDRANGER 186/187

WHITES COPSE

GATE

POND

N

SONGHURST FARM

SCALE 1:25000

ALFORD PH

ALFORD BARS

PH

OAKHURST FARM

CONTINUED FROM MAP 18

BARBERRY BRIDGE

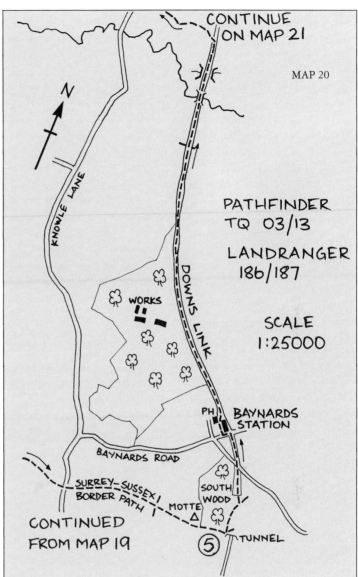

the seventeenth century to secure a parliamentary bill but it was not until 1813 that it was finally successful. Barges from the coast brought seaweed for fertilizers, grain for milling and a wide variety of groceries and goods for the village stores and they returned loaded with farm produce. Cobden farm in Sydney Wood had its own private wharf and a brickworks was established on the northern bank once the canal was built.

During its short working life, the canal failed to attract much trade and suffered from poor water retention. Ulti-

Sunlight near Baynards Station.

mately, the Guildford to Horsham railway destroyed its viability and the canal was forced to close in 1871 with the land and buildings gradually being sold back to riparian owners.

The Wey–Arun Canal Trust, a group of enthusiastic volunteers, have restored sections of the canal in recent years.

2 *Old Lock house*

The Old Lock house lies to the R of the path and was the canal companies' main workshops where lock gates were made and repaired. In the mid-nineteenth century, John Coles, who was the master carpenter, lived there with his family for over 30 years. The house is now in private ownership.

3 *Glass Industry*

Activity in this woodland pre-dates the canal. Along with other woods in the Chiddingfold area, it was at the centre of a local glass-making industry as early as the fourteenth century. Using locally available sand from Hambledon, ash from bracken for flux and imported lime, the primitive barrel-shaped furnaces containing the fireproof crucibles were set in the local clay. Fragments of these crucibles and pieces of window glass and bottles have been found at several sites within Sydney Wood. It seems that the glass industry survived in the Wealden forests from the break up of the Roman Empire until the early 1600s when it could no longer compete with the new coal-fired furnaces in the Midlands.

The name 'Glass House Copse' remains and the old coppice woodland seen around this route are reminders of the times when charcoal fuelled the glass furnaces.

4 *Locks*

Protracted negotiations with landowners led to the routing of the canal through Sydney Wood, to avoid their game reserves. This lengthened the summit level by 3 miles (5 km) and added £15,000 to the estimated cost.

From its highest point in Sydney Wood, the canal descended through a series of closely-spaced locks. Since the canal closed in 1871, these have been blown up for demolition practice leaving only steep changes in level to mark their former locations.

5 *Downs Link Bridleway*

The Downs Link Bridleway and the Sussex Border Path run parallel here for a short distance.

The boundary bank between the counties of Surrey and Sussex lies to the north of the path and in the field ahead oak trees planted in pairs in Victorian times mark the continuation of the county boundary. Unfortunately, they suffered damage during the 1987 storm.

The Guildford to Horsham railway was built as a single

Sydney Wood – a typical Wealden woodland.

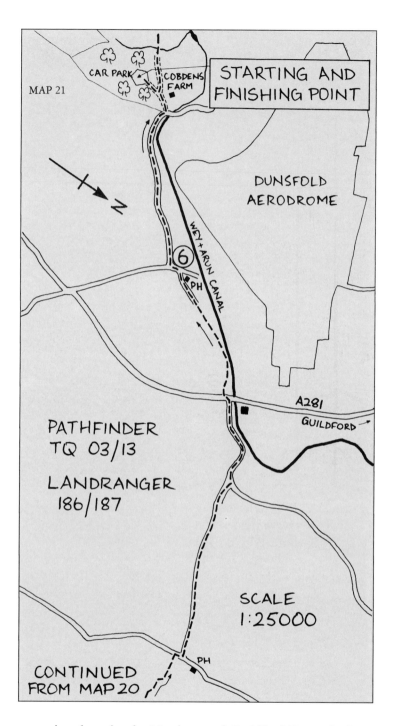

track railway by the Horsham and Guildford Direct Railway Company and ran from Guildford to Christ's Hospital where it connected with the line from Shoreham to Itchingfield junction. It was opened in 1865, but by 1966 Dr Beeching, a government adviser, had recommended its closure.

A joint project between Surrey and West Sussex County

A signpost on the Downs Link.

Councils and Waverley Borough Council led to its reopening as a long distance bridleway linking the North Downs Way to the South Downs Way in 1984.

The beautifully-restored Baynards' station is now in private ownership. Closeby are the gates to the Baynards' estate with its formal, tree-lined drive. The Thurlow Arms public house was built by a former owner of Baynards Manor who had allowed the railway to be built on his land.

6 *Dunsfold Aerodrome*

The Three Compasse's public house hosted the official opening celebrations of the canal in 1816 and offered hospitality to many bargees. A $2^1/_2$ mile (4 km) conduit from Vachery pond, near Cranleigh, flowed into the canal south of Fastwater and was the canal's only regular supply of water. This, however, was insufficient and in dry periods goods often had to be taken overland between Alfold and Cranleigh.

The road past the public house used to be the main road between Cranleigh and Alfold before the bypass to the east was built in 1942 to skirt Dunsfold aerodrome.

3·14

THE TRUNDLE AND HEYSHOTT DOWN

STARTING AND FINISHING
POINT
Car-park west of the Trundle, 1
mile (1.6 km) south of Singleton
which is on the A286
(SU 81/91–871110).
LENGTH
11 miles (18 km)
ASCENT
1100 ft (340 m)

This scenic walk visits the Trundle with fine views across the coastal plain. Passing the attractive, flint-built village of Singleton, it climbs to the crest of the Downs and returns through the Charlton Forest and past Goodwood Country Park.

ROUTE DESCRIPTION (Maps 22–24)

From the car-park, follow the track up towards the radio masts to the top of the Trundle (1) with fine views of Chichester and the harbour beyond. Go ahead towards the iron railings and turn L downhill on steep path with railings on R. Cross road to go through parking area and along road towards Charlton. Go half L over stile and follow posts, and then fence, across field towards Singleton (2). Keep ahead on path into Singleton churchyard and turn R between wall and hedge.

Turn L along lane to reach road, and turn R. In 25 yards (23 m) turn L up fenced track and along headland to go half R across field to two stiles. Keep ahead up open grass slope to gate in the fence line. Follow the path around Levin Down to gate and at signpost turn L along fenced track towards Heyshott. At track junction, Burnt Oak Gate, keep ahead up track into woodland, ignoring all cross-tracks. At top of scarp, turn R, joining SDW. Detour L to the OS trig point on Heyshott Downs for a splendid view over the Weald towards the pine-clad hills of Hindhead and Blackdown. Return to route.

Keep ahead to pass tumuli (Bronze Age barrows), on the L. After Graffham Conservation area on R, turn R on to cross-track and follow downhill ignoring all other cross-tracks. Go through gate into field and down to field corner. Cross track and go half R up grass path and over stile. Continue over field to woods at top. Cross stile and keep ahead up track. At T-junction turn R on track and continue down road. Look for, and turn R alongside hedge. Turn L along road towards houses and at T-junction turn R.

At the pond, keep ahead along road to Goodwood. In 50 yards

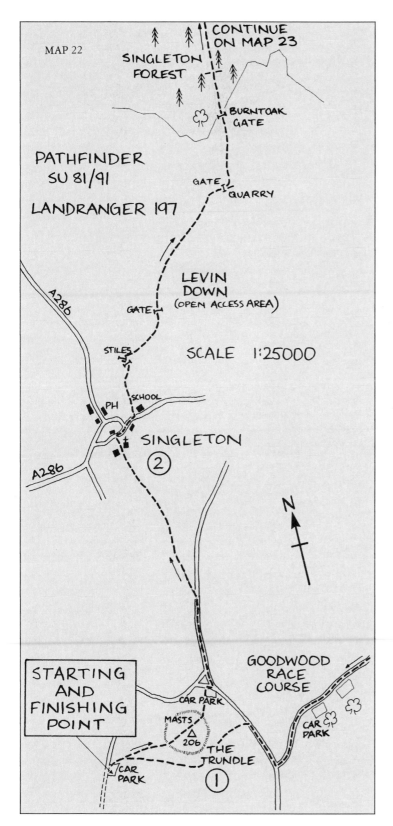

MAP 22

CONTINUE
ON MAP 23

SINGLETON
FOREST

BURNTOAK
GATE

PATHFINDER
SU 81/91

LANDRANGER 197

GATE

QUARRY

LEVIN
DOWN
(OPEN ACCESS AREA)

GATE

STILES

SCALE 1:25000

PH

SCHOOL

SINGLETON
②

A286

A286

N

STARTING
AND
FINISHING
POINT

GOODWOOD
RACE
COURSE

CAR PARK

MASTS

△ 206

CAR
PARK

THE
TRUNDLE
①

CAR
PARK

Flint faced walls in Singleton.

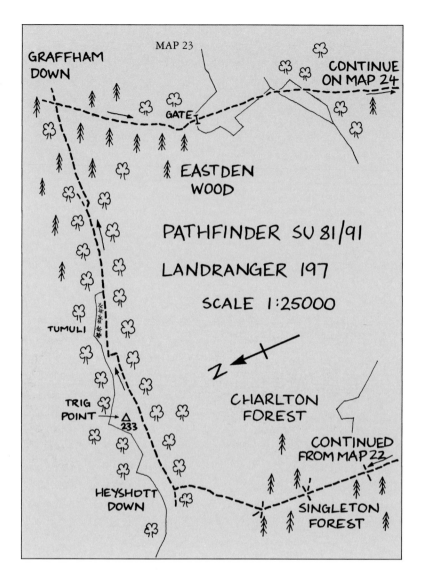

(45 m) turn R on track and follow fence on R to field corner. Cross stile and go half L uphill to wood. Keep ahead through wood and open area to gate and follow track to road. Turn R along grass verge and at T-junction turn R towards Singleton. Opposite west entrance to Goodwood racecourse *(3)* turn L and then L again onto track alongside iron railings. Keep ahead around the Trundle back to car-park.

1 The Trundle

The name Trundle comes from the Anglo-Saxon 'trendle', meaning a loop or circle which aptly describes this summit hillfort. Occupying such a prominent position it could hardly fail to attract early settlers. It was permanently occupied by Neolithic farmers who, keeping pigs, sheep and cattle, dug a

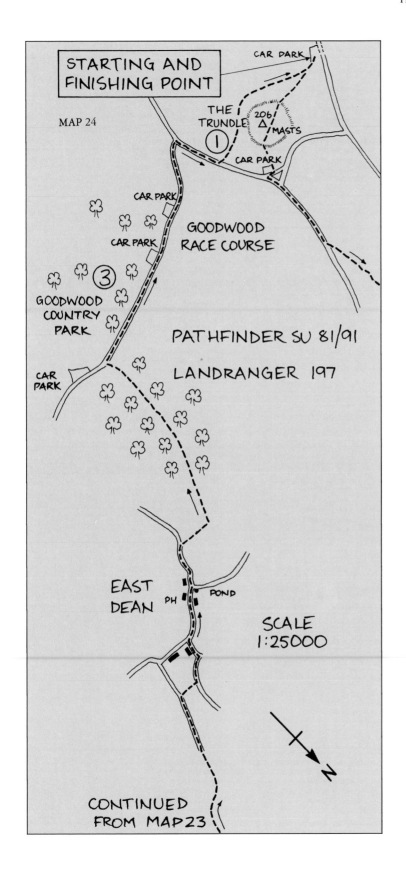

STARTING AND
FINISHING POINT

CAR PARK

MAP 24

THE
TRUNDLE
①
206 △ MASTS

CAR PARK

CAR PARK

CAR PARK

GOODWOOD
RACE COURSE

③

GOODWOOD
COUNTRY
PARK

CAR
PARK

PATHFINDER SU 81/91

LANDRANGER 197

EAST
DEAN
PH POND

SCALE
1:25000

N

CONTINUED
FROM MAP 23

series of ditches around the summit of the hill – a causewayed camp. Later, during the Iron Age, the hillfort was built around this camp. The remains of a high, earthen bank, formed from the spoil of a deep ditch enclosing some 13 acres (5.3 ha) of hilltop, can clearly be seen. There were timber gateways on the west and east sides and defence was completed with a timber palisade around the top of the bank. In medieval times, Saint Roches Chapel which was within the parish of Singleton, stood on the summit of the Trundle but it fell into ruins centuries ago. Immediately below the hillfort is Goodwood race course.

2 *Singleton*

This lovely, flint village with a large, castellated tower to its church lies below a steep face of the South Downs. The knapped flints facing many buildings are characteristic of Downland villages. In this area, early man relied upon flint for his tools and weapons. Flint flakes were used to scrape skins and fashion wooden tools.

An entry in the Domesday book records 'Silletone' (which may have come from an Old English name for brushwood, or a thicket), as a thriving community with two mills, enough land for 80 ploughs and 150 hogs. The present, part Saxon, church was the central church of the Hundred of Singleton owned by the great Earl of Godwin, father of King Harold who died at the battle of Hastings in 1066.

3 *Goodwood*

Horse racing, sometimes called the 'Sport of Kings', has flourished on the Downs and is as popular now as when racing began. The first three-day meeting at Goodwood was held in April 1802. A grandstand seating 3000 people was built in 1832 and now there are three meets annually.

The Midhurst–Chichester branch of the London, Brighton and South Coast Railway opened in 1881 and carried race horses and many race goers, greatly swelling the local population on race days. A splendid station, lavishly adorned with marble, was built between Singleton and West Dean, with an eye to the lucrative Goodwood traffic. It is now a winery.

Goodwood House, the historic seat of the Dukes of Richmond and Gordon and the home of generations of the Gordon-Lennox family, lies to the south. With its fine collection of pictures and furniture it is well worth a visit, although the functional flint finish is unusual for such an aristocratic building. It was the 3rd Duke of Richmond who was responsible for rebuilding the house.

Barley on Heyshott Down.

DITCHLING BEACON AND WOLSTONBURY HILL

STARTING AND FINISHING
POINT
Windmill car-park signposted
along Mill Lane, 9 miles (14 km)
north of Brighton near the village
of Clayton, signed off the A273,
north of the junction of the A23
and A273 at Pyecombe
(TQ 21/31–303133).
LENGTH
12 miles (19 km), or 8 miles
(13 km) using the link path
between A–B
ASCENT
1775 ft (540 m)

This superb Downland walk visits two of the classic viewpoints of the South Downs, Jack and Jill windmills and Ditchling Beacon, and two of the lesser known, Wolstonbury and Newtimber Hill. There are splendid views along the Downland ridge westwards and from Newtimber Hill into the Devil's Dyke.

ROUTE DESCRIPTION (Maps 25, 26)

Pass windmills (1) on R to go through gate in corner of car-park. Turn L and then L again alongside fence and follow path down through gates to road. Turn L past Clayton church (2) to road and at T-junction turn R over railway (3). Turn L along road and then L again up drive to 'Warenne'. Pass flint barn on R and keep ahead up track. Turn R over stile to skirt quarry and follow fence on L up to Wolstonbury Hill (4) with views of Danny down below R and Chanctonbury Ring ahead.

Turn L from the OS trig point across the top of the hill, over stile to reach track. Turn L with windmills in distance on L and then keep ahead through gates. Turn R on cross-track. In 100 yards (90 m) (A) turn R over stile and bear L around field (path may be indistinct) to stile. Go half R down through scrub to stile and half R again down across field towards farm buildings. Go diagonally across farm track, look for stile and go down path to road. Turn R along road and opposite The Street turn L across road. Ignore track beside buildings and go up parallel, stepped path and keep ahead up slope with fence on L. Pass fence and turn R along it. Go through gate and continue through, and beside woodland strip. With gorse on R go through second gate and keep ahead through open scrub on Newtimber Hill (5), to pass fenced dew pond on L. Bear L in wide arc around top of hill and keep ahead down track with quarry on R. There is an excellent view of the Devil's Dyke.

Turn L over stile, joining SDW, pass buildings and go up path through gates to top of slope. Keep ahead, alongside field, and

The Jill windmill.

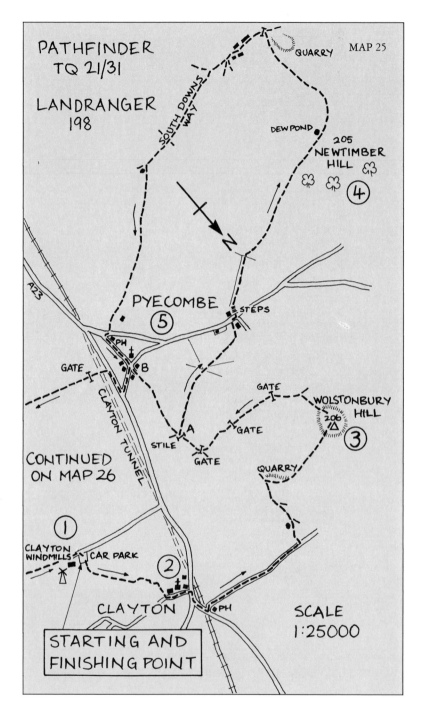

bear L down to road. Cross A23 and bear L along Church Lane.
Detour L at T-junction to visit Pycombe church *(6)* and return to
route. Turn R along School Lane and at T-junction turn R along
road, leaving SDW. In 125 yards (110 m) turn L and follow track
up across golf course with windmills away to L. Keep ahead to
eventually turn R through hedge and past barn. Before buildings,

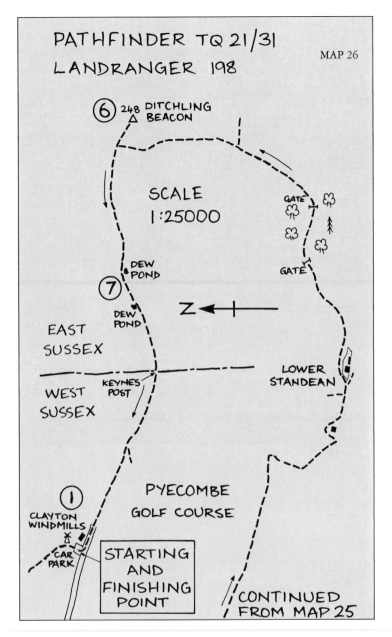

PATHFINDER TQ 21/31
LANDRANGER 198

MAP 26

⑥ 248 DITCHLING BEACON

SCALE 1:25000

DEW POND

⑦

DEW POND

Z ←

EAST SUSSEX

WEST SUSSEX

KEYNES POST

GATE

GATE

LOWER STANDEAN

PYECOMBE GOLF COURSE

① CLAYTON WINDMILLS

CAR PARK

STARTING AND FINISHING POINT

CONTINUED FROM MAP 25

Clayton tunnel.

turn L up track and bear R down and L along valley floor. Look for gate on R and keep ahead, alongside fence. Bear L through gate up to trees at head of valley and follow track up to crest of ridge. Detour R to visit Ditchling Beacon *(7)* and return to route.

Turn L along the ridge, past dew ponds and chalk heath *(8)*. Keep ahead past the Keymer Post topped with an acorn finial. Bear R on cross-track and turn R to car-park.

1 Jack and Jill
One hundred years ago, windmills were a common sight on

the Downs but with the coming of steam power only a few now remain. Situated on the Downs above Clayton, the contrasting Jack and Jill windmills worked together until 1906. Jill, the older of the two, is a white-timbered post-mill. The mill body is automatically turned by a fan tackle to keep the sweeps facing the wind. She was built in Brighton in 1821 and dragged here across the Downs by teams of oxen. Following extensive restoration and quick thinking during the 1987 storm by members of the Jack and Jill Windmill Preservation Society, Jill is working again producing stone-ground, wholemeal flour. Jack, a black, brick-built tower-mill, is in private ownership.

2 *Clayton*

Clayton, a typical springline settlement, lies at the foot of the steep scarp face of the Downs. Its church has a fine, moulded Saxon chancel arch and an impressive series of twelfth-century wall paintings depicting the Last Judgement. These were only discovered at the beginning of this century. They are examples of true frescos where the colour was painted onto wet plaster and were used to teach the Gospel stories when most people could not read or write.

3 *Railway Tunnel*

The London and Brighton Railway, which opened in 1841, enters a $1\frac{1}{2}$ mile (2.5 km) long tunnel through the Downs here. The tunnel entrance is an interesting example of Victorian Gothic architecture and incorporates a cottage in its turreted northern portal. The line revolutionized travel between the Weald and the South coast.

4 *Wolstonbury Hill*

The rounded Wolstonbury Hill is capped by an unusual oval Iron Age hillfort. The entrance was on the south side but can no longer be seen. Within, is an earlier Iron Age enclosure and more recent chalk pits.

Lying to the north, Danny, an impressive manor house, can be glimpsed in parkland below the Downs. The southern face of the house, like its interior, is early eighteenth century but the eastern elevation is Elizabethan.

5 *Newtimber Hill and the Devil's Dyke*

Rain water filters through the porous chalk and so ponds do not form on the Downs. It was not until the eighteenth century that dew ponds were built to provide water for grazing animals. Sheep, in fact, require very little water and could satisfy their needs when they were folded in the valley over

The north scarp of the South Downs.

night. Traditionally, dew ponds were lined with flint and puddled clay but nowadays concrete is often used. Most are a saucer shape with sloping sides to funnel rainwater to replenish them. Despite the name, water droplets in dew do not contribute significantly to water levels.

From Newtimber Hill there is a magnificent view into the Devil's Dyke, a deep gash cut into the face of the Downs which turns a right angle a third of the way through. It is a very deep, dry valley but was said to be the Devil's own work to let the sea into the Weald to drown all the churches. He fled leaving his task undone when he mistook the light of a candle held by an old woman looking out of her window for the first glimpse of sunrise. A branch line of the Brighton to Portsmouth railway ran to Devil's Dyke farm until 1938. For a short time around the turn of the century, visitors could take a cable car across the Dyke and a funicular railway down the scarp to visit Poynings.

6 *Pyecombe*

The celebrated shepherd's crook, used for catching sheep by the neck or leg, was once made in the quiet village of Pyecombe. But the decline in sheep grazing inevitably marked the end of this local industry. The church contains an unusual lead font decorated with intricate script and the gate into the churchyard with a crook for a latch recalls the traditional craft.

7 *Ditchling Beacon*

Ditchling Beacon, an Iron Age hillfort, was one of a chain of summits on which beacon fires were lit to warn off the Armada four centuries ago. Nestling at the foot of the Downs lies the lovely village of Ditchling. Sixty years ago, Ditchling became well-known for the artists and craftsmen who settled there, inspired by the landscape. Edward Johnston (1872–1944) gained international fame with his revival of the medieval art of lettering. His innovative block alphabet is still used by London Transport today. Also living there was Eric Gill (1882–1940) who started the Ditchling press, famous for its wallpaper and furniture design. It still survives today but is no longer based in Ditchling.

3·16

ASHDOWN FOREST AND WITHYHAM

STARTING AND FINISHING POINT
Station Road car-park, Forest Row, which is signed off the B2110 near its junction with the A22 (TQ 43/53–426352).
LENGTH
15 miles (24 km)
ASCENT
700 ft (210 m)
ALTERNATIVE ROUTE
By following Route 1 from B round to A, the Enchanted Place and Four Counties Dial can be visited and the walk extended to 16 miles (26 km).

The walk starts gently along the trackbed of a disused railway before climbing up through trees to circuit the sandy heights of the Ashdown Forest, the highest part of the central Weald. From here there are expansive views across the Weald to the escarpments of the North and South Downs. In summer, the purple flowering heather and the yellow gorse is a delightful sight. In dry weather there is a significant fire risk in this area. Please DO NOT light fires or drop cigarettes or matches.

ROUTE DESCRIPTION (Maps 27–30)

Turn L out of car-park then L along Station Road. Pass to L of social club, go through gap in laurel hedge and turn R along track. In 75 yards (69 m), turn R through gate to meet and follow trackbed of old railway, now the Forest Way Country Park (1). Go under two bridges and 2 miles (3.2 km) later, go over wooden rail bridge. In 250 yards (228 m) turn R over stile and follow path ahead along field edges and to R of tennis courts to reach Hartfield. Turn R along road then L to pass The Anchor and parish church (2).

Turn R over stile opposite porch of church and bear L across field. Cross next field, go over stiles and go ahead across field to stile. Bear R across large field aiming to R of trees and to L of church on knoll. Cross stile down in far R corner and turn R on road. Turn R up road to Withyham church (3) to meet and follow WW.

Keep ahead along private road to Buckhurst Farm. At gate across road, turn L on fenced path. Enter Five Hundred Acre Wood (4), crossing the line of the medieval park pale. Go ahead on track, swing R past cottage and bear R on track to go downhill. Pass pond on R then, at top of rise, turn L on wide track going uphill through the woods. Bear R with main track and later go over cross-track and stile and ahead up path through old woodland. Near top, join main track then soon bear R to go gradually

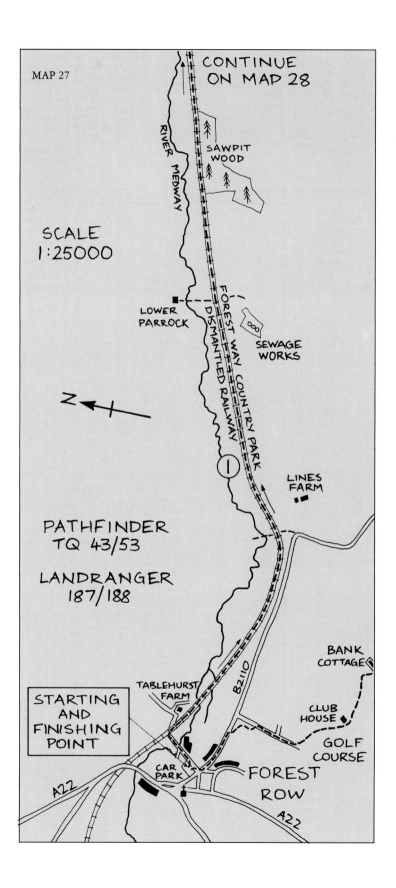

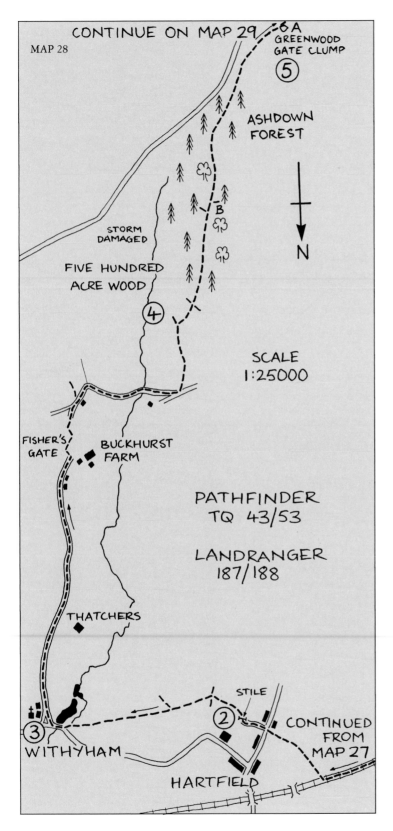

MAP 28

CONTINUE ON MAP 29

6 A
GREENWOOD
GATE CLUMP
⑤

ASHDOWN
FOREST

B

N

STORM
DAMAGED

FIVE HUNDRED
ACRE WOOD

④

SCALE
1:25000

PATHFINDER
TQ 43/53

LANDRANGER
187/188

FISHER'S
GATE

BUCKHURST
FARM

THATCHERS

STILE

②

CONTINUED
FROM
MAP 27

③

WITHYHAM

HARTFIELD

Withyham Church, built from local sandstone.

uphill across Ashdown Forest. Bear R on wide track (past B) and follow, ignoring tracks off. Pass Greenwood Gate Clump *(5)* on R (and A) and keep ahead over cross-track. Cross road to car-park to L of private road to Old Lodge. Follow path along R-side of car-park, go over cross-track and keep straight ahead to reach Camp Hill Clump.

Go over cross-track, leaving WW, and follow wide track passing a pond and three car-parks on L and Friends Clump planted in 1973 to mark 'The Year of the Tree' on R. At house, go to L of wide track to follow path around boundary on L. Turn L over stile to visit Nutley Windmill, a nineteenth-century post-mill restored by the Nutley Preservation Society between 1969 and 1972. Go back over stile and downhill to turn L along the broad track. Follow downhill through gate, bearing R then L to cross stream and follow track uphill. At top, turn R alongside fence in front of Millbrook Clump then bear L through gate and along path.

Cross road and follow track to R of car-park to go parallel to road on R. Cross minor road then, nearly 750 yards (686 m) later, look for broad track on L and turn R on small path opposite this to cross road to end of houses. Go through gateway to R of house, along track, over stile and past old stables. Follow path ahead over fields and then along track, crossing land enclosed from Ashdown Forest in 1693. Go past Ashdown Park on R *(6)*, turn R on entrance drive, then go through car-park and up grassy path to road. To visit Ashdown Forest Centre *(7)*, turn R on road. Return to route.

Cross road to go down road to Broadstone Farm opposite. About 50 yards (45 m) before farm gate, bear L through trees to meet and follow track which meanders gently down through storm-damaged woodland and then along edge of golf course. At start of houses on R, turn L over grass to go down shallow valley. Turn L on track through trees and keep along track to pass clubhouse of Royal Ashdown Forest Golf Club on R and reach road. Turn R down road then L on fenced path just past Herons Wood. Turn L along road and R to Station Road car-park.

1 Forest Way Country Park
The Forest Way is a linear Country Park managed by East Sussex County Council. It follows a disused, single-track railway which ran for 9½ miles (15.5 km) from the outskirts of Groombridge to East Grinstead. The line was opened in 1866 by the London, Brighton and South Coast Railway and closed in 1966 as part of the Beeching cuts.

The Ashdown Forest from the Weald Way.

To the L of the track is the valley of the infant River Medway which was navigable in medieval times transporting iron and timber from the Weald to London.

2 *St Mary the Virgin, Hartfield*

The church, built of local sandstone, dates from the thirteenth century and the shingle spire, characteristic of the area, was added 200 years later. The timber-framed Lychgate Cottage is one of the oldest buildings in the village.

3 *Withyham*

The medieval church of St Michael and All Angels was almost completely destroyed when struck by lightning in 1663. The rebuilt church was then heavily restored by the Victorians. The Sackville Chapel houses many monuments to one of the few families who can genuinely trace their ancestors back to Norman times when Herbrand de Sauqueville of Normandy crossed the Channel with William the Conqueror. The poet and novelist Vita Sackville-West (1892–1962) is buried in the family chapel. Seventeenth-century iron railings in the chapel, and the iron grave slab at the west end of the nave, are a reminder of the once extensive Wealden Iron Industry.

4 *Five Hundred Acre Wood and Ashdown Forest*

The wood was enclosed from Ashdown Forest in 1693 (see page 24). The lower slopes are planted with softwoods and there are older beech and oak trees in the upper part of the wood. The woods were badly affected by the 1987 storm and clearance and new planting can be seen. During 1988–89 over 3000 trees, mainly beech and oak, were planted around the Ashdown Forest to replace those lost.

5 *Greenwood Gate Clump*

The Clumps, see page 26.

6 *Ashdown Park*

This vast mansion was built in 1867. Additions, including a large Gothic chapel, were built in 1924 when it became a convent. More recently it served as a film set for *Escape from Colditz*. It is now a management training centre.

7 *Ashdown Forest Centre*

The Ashdown Forest Rangers are based in the Forest Centre. This 300-year-old, timber-framed barn was re-erected from Hassocks in East Sussex and, with its excellent interpretive displays, forms a focal point for the management of the Forest. East Sussex County Council now own the Forest and the Forest Rangers, helped by Conservation Volunteers, manage the area for recreation and conservation. As has happened on so many ancient heaths, the commoners, with rare exceptions, no longer exercise their traditional rights and this has inevitably led to the spread of birch and pine.

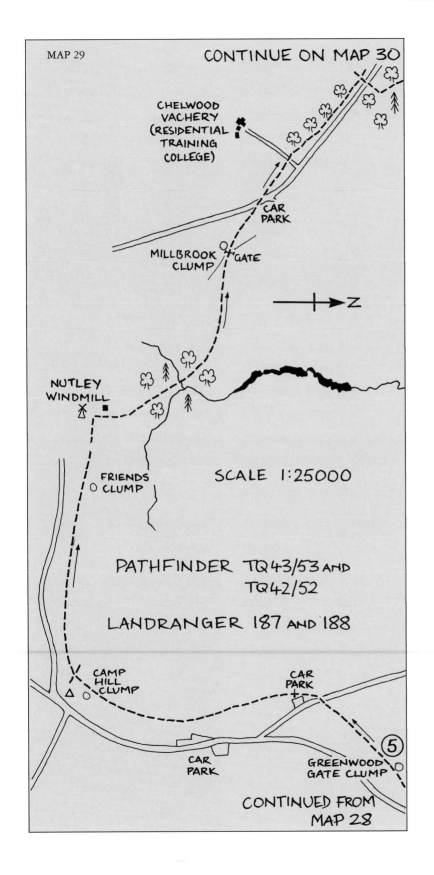

MAP 29

CONTINUE ON MAP 30

CHELWOOD VACHERY (RESIDENTIAL TRAINING COLLEGE)

CAR PARK

MILLBROOK CLUMP

GATE

Z

NUTLEY WINDMILL

FRIENDS CLUMP

SCALE 1:25000

PATHFINDER TQ 43/53 AND TQ42/52

LANDRANGER 187 AND 188

CAMP HILL CLUMP

CAR PARK

CAR PARK

⑤

GREENWOOD GATE CLUMP

CONTINUED FROM MAP 28

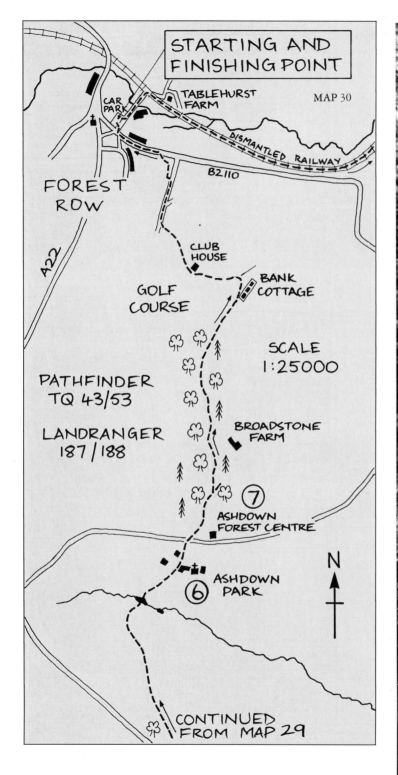

The 500 Acre Wood.

MIDHURST AND PETWORTH

A delightful walk across the Greensand. It features the attractive landscaped Park at Petworth and the picturesque ruins of Cowdray House and returns over the sandy heath and woodlands of Ambersham, and Duncton Commons.

STARTING AND FINISHING POINT

Petworth Park NT car-park signed off A283, north of the Park. Gates open 9 am and shut at 9 pm, or dusk if earlier. A donation is requested. Dogs must be kept under proper control to avoid disturbing sheep and deer (su 82/92–966238).

LENGTH

17 miles (27 km)

ASCENT

525 ft (160 m)

ROUTE DESCRIPTION (Maps 31–34)

From entrance to car-park, go ahead through trees and Petworth Park *(1)* to reach lodge and turn L along track. Pass tall folly on far R and 275 yards (250 m) after tree planting on L, turn R up shallow valley to corner of wall. Go through gates to road and turn R along road through Upperton, an attractive hamlet built almost entirely of the mellow local sandstone. At T-junction, turn L down lane and bear R up drive to 'Woodgers'. Keep the house on the L and just before white gate turn R and then L around field edge. Cross road and keep ahead over field with Pitshill House *(2)* ahead.

Turn R up access drive and over cattle grid. At house on L fork R down grassy path and in 30 yards (27 m), immediately after overhead cable, look for and turn L on narrow path, from where there are glimpses over to Lurgershall NT Commons. By wall, cross track, go over stile and down stepped path to road. Turn L and then R over stile down through garden and keep ahead. After larch plantation, look for path and bear R off main track down towards stream and over bridge. Go half R across field to keep wood on R and go ahead on track into wood. At Y-junction, bear L and ahead over footbridge into field. Keep ahead, with hedge on L and bear L beside wall to road. Turn L along road and R by village hall and then turn R again up road, past Oakfields. Bear L up stoney track and keep ahead ignoring all tracks off. At T-junction, turn R on track past Upper Vining and ahead on grassy track. In 30 yards (27 m), turn L up bank by farm building and keep ahead on track. Go over cross-track and then turn L along R-side of field. Before field corner, turn R over stile and keep ahead along L-edge

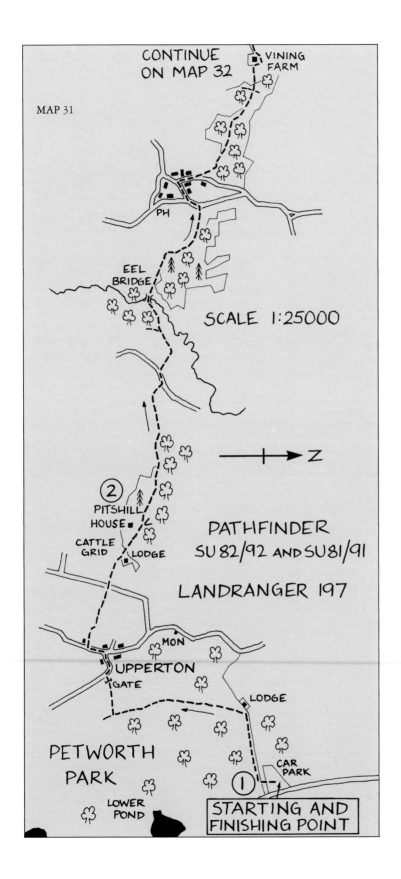

CONTINUE
ON MAP 32

VINING
FARM

MAP 31

PH

EEL
BRIDGE

SCALE 1:25000

⊢——▶ Z

②
PITSHILL
HOUSE

PATHFINDER
SU 82/92 AND SU 81/91

CATTLE
GRID

LODGE

LANDRANGER 197

MON

UPPERTON
GATE

LODGE

PETWORTH
PARK

CAR
PARK

①

LOWER
POND

STARTING AND
FINISHING POINT

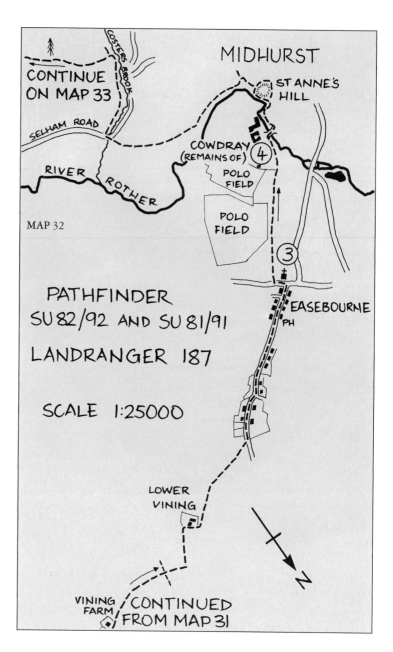

MAP 32

PATHFINDER
SU 82/92 AND SU 81/91

LANDRANGER 187

SCALE 1:25000

of field. Turn L around garden and ahead along track and farm drive to road. Turn L and then L again past church at Easebourne *(3)*. Turn R along drive beside church and keep ahead with polo fields and ruins of Cowdray House *(4)* on L. Detour from route to visit ruins.

At old entrance gates, turn R over stone bridge and L along river and through gate. Where path swings L beside river, go ahead up stepped path and detour L up bank to St Anne's Hill. Return to route and either go straight ahead to visit Midhurst or turn L at wooden fence and follow path downhill. Turn R over stone-arched bridge. Turn L around house and keep ahead on path, track and then access drive through stables. Continue along road and in 30 yards (27 m) turn R along wide sandy track. After conifer plantation, turn L ignoring all turnings off. Turn L at T-junction and then R on cross-track. Then, 25 yards (23 m) after track swings L, turn R on path down bank and over footbridge. Bear R uphill on narrow path and at top of gulley turn R and go ahead under brick arch bridge. At houses, turn L on track to road. Cross and bear R on path. Bear L on sandy track and keep ahead along wide, sandy track.

Pass OS trig point and where track swings R, ignore path ahead and bear R along narrow path down to stream. Keep ahead, ignoring L-fork and turn L on sandy track. Turn R at T-junction and keep ahead. Swing L with track and keep ahead. Go along field edge and after second gate, bear R across field, through gate and ahead up sandy track. Look for, and bear L on to, sandy path and go straight over road. After passing through boundary bank, turn L at T-junction. Cross road and keep ahead on sandy access track. Just before track forks, turn R on sandy track then swing L with track and keep ahead. Swing R with track over river to road. Turn L, and just before road becomes track, turn R on track. Bear L through boundary bank and keep ahead. Bear L at T-junction and keep ahead to road. Turn L along road and after bridge turn L up lane and then ahead up track to footbridge. Turn L beside house and go through two gates. Immediately after ditch, turn R over stile along field edge. Keep ahead on track which swings R and then go across field, keeping hedge and house on R. Bear R along track and at farm turn L down farm drive. Cross road and go ahead up road to Upperton, passing church *(5)*. Where road swings L, turn R back into Petworth Park. Turn L along track and bear R back to car-park.

1 Petworth House

The skilfully landscaped park at Petworth reconciles the less than beautiful house by creating sweeping vistas of grassland grazed by deer with a serpentine lake framed by clumps of limes, planes and sweet chestnut trees. The deer park has one of the largest herds of fallow deer in the country. Many of the great parks were reshaped in the eighteenth century under the influence of Capability Brown but Petworth was designed by him personally at the invitation of Lord Egremont, its owner. Follies, a feature of this period, abound. The turreted Gothic tower, standing on a rise just within the west wall of the park, was built about 1800 to provide a focus for the view from Petworth House. It is now a private residence.

Turner was a frequent visitor to Petworth and immortalized

Petworth House.

some of this idyllic landscape in paintings which hang in the house. There has always been a house on this site since 1309 but it was Charles Seymour, the 6th Duke of Somerset, who set about rebuilding it in 1688. The only remains of the original house are walls of the chapel and undercroft. A white marble copy of Michelangelo's Pieta stands in a niche marking the position of the medieval west window of the chapel.

The town of Petworth, which appears to cling to the side of the estate, is worth a visit, too, despite the ever-present traffic.

2 Pitshill House

Pitshill House stands at the head of a small valley with a view to the Downs beyond. The rhododendrons and azaleas in the beautifully landscaped gardens are a riot of colour in spring. Until 1944 it was the home of the Mitford family. The track goes through a sandstone cutting and the stone has been used to build a retaining wall under the root ball of a huge beech that toppled in the 1987 storm.

3 Easebourne Priory and St Anne's Hill

Little is known of the fortified manor house which once stood on St Anne's Hill, Midhurst, but it included a hall, chapel and other buildings. It is thought that in about 1248 one of the de Bohun family living in the manor, founded a Priory for ten Benedictine nuns and their prioress at Easebourne.

The east end of Easebourne church was rebuilt to provide private worship for the nuns, and the parishioners were accommodated by widening the north aisle, so creating two churches under one roof. The buildings of the former priory are now incorporated into a private house although traces of the cloister wall can be seen.

The church contains an alabaster memorial to Sir David Owen who married the heiress Mary de Bohun. He died in 1535 and left generous endowments to the church and priory in his will. He is thought to have been the natural son of Owen Tudor, grandfather of Henry VII.

Over the centuries, the nuns gained a reputation for extravagance and in 1441 great exception was taken to the prioress's excessive expenditure on furs, jewels and lap dogs and at the time of the dissolution in 1535, Henry VIII confiscated Sir David's endowments, dismantled the priory and gave it to Sir William Fitzwilliam, the owner of Cowdray House.

Opposite the priory is a gateless lych gate. It was once a cattle grid and private bypass bridge for motors not exceeding two tons and the old inscription remains.

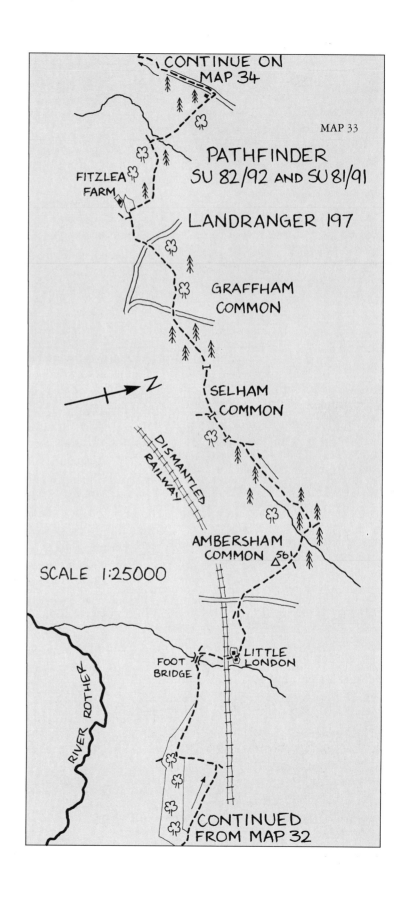

CONTINUE ON
MAP 34

MAP 33

PATHFINDER
SU 82/92 AND SU 81/91

LANDRANGER 197

FITZLEA
FARM

GRAFFHAM
COMMON

Z

SELHAM
COMMON

DISMANTLED
RAILWAY

AMBERSHAM
COMMON △561

SCALE 1:25000

FOOT
BRIDGE

LITTLE
LONDON

RIVER ROTHER

CONTINUED
FROM MAP 32

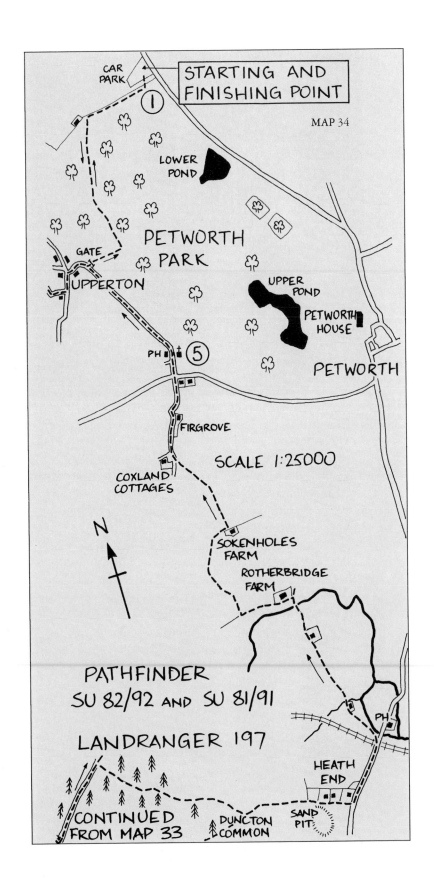

STARTING AND FINISHING POINT

CAR PARK

①

MAP 34

LOWER POND

PETWORTH PARK

GATE

UPPERTON

UPPER POND

PETWORTH HOUSE

PETWORTH

PH ⑤

FIRGROVE

SCALE 1:25000

COXLAND COTTAGES

N

SOKENHOLES FARM

ROTHERBRIDGE FARM

PATHFINDER SU 82/92 AND SU 81/91

LANDRANGER 197

PH

HEATH END

CONTINUED FROM MAP 33

DUNCTON COMMON

SAND PIT

The ruins of Cowdray House.

4 *Midhurst: Cowdray Park and Cowdray House*
The delightful town of Midhurst has retained considerable character and, lying adjacent to the town, Cowdray Park with its 600 acres (243 hectares) of rolling parkland is famous throughout the world for polo. A raised causeway leads from the town to the ruins of one of Tudor England's most magnificent fortified houses.

Cowdray House was built in the reign of Henry VIII on the site of a medieval manor and was owned by the Montague family. Over the centuries, the family suffered great misfortune: in September 1793 the house, with all its priceless pictures and treasures, was gutted by fire, and the following month the young heir was drowned while abroad. In 1815, there was further tragedy when his sister's two young sons were also drowned.

5 *All Hallows Church, Tillington*
The crowned heads that greet you, on each side of the door, as you enter this church are just one of the indelible marks that Lord Egremont left on this church. Far more radical was the rebuilding of the tower topped with a 'Scot's crown spire'. The tower is one storey too large for the church but it is an impressive sight when seen from Petworth Park. Within the church, there are numerous memorials to the Mitford family of Pitshill including one marking the recovery, not death, of William Slade Mitford, aged 11, from an accident in 1909.

HASCOMBE AND HYDON'S BALL

Car-park adjacent to former
Bramley and Wonersh station,
Station Road, Bramley, off the
A281 (TQ 04/14–010451).
Alternative start for 9¹/₂ mile
(15 km) circuit is Winkworth
Arboretum NT car-park on the
B2130 Godalming to Hascombe
road (SU 84 / 94–989411). A
donation is requested.

LENGTH

15 miles (24 km). A 5-mile (8-km)
circuit can be walked by leaving
the outward route at A and
turning R back to Bramley.
Alternatively, by starting at
Winkworth and following the
return route to A and then turning
R on the outward route a 9¹/₂ mile
(15 km) circuit can be followed.

ASCENT

1050 ft (320 m)

This is a very scenic and varied walk at any time of year but it is especially recommended in the spring, when the woods are car-
peted with bluebells and the azalea steps in Winkworth
Arboretum are a mass of colour, and in the autumn when the
Arboretum's maples are a blaze of red.

ROUTE DESCRIPTION (Maps 35–38)

From car-park, cross road to go through gate and along the
trackbed of a former railway, the Downs Link Bridleway *(1)*.
Where this runs along an embankment, the derelict Wey–Arun
canal and the Bramley stream which fed it can be seen to the L.
Immediately before first bridge over bridleway, turn R up steps
then R on track, joining GW. Turn L along road then R in front of
house to follow field edge. Pass house and go ahead along road.
Where this turns L, turn R to follow track, later bearing L (A),
briefly meeting the return route.

Turn R over stile opposite barn on L, and follow field edge
uphill. Pass barn, then cross stile and gate and keep ahead up
across field, through gap and downhill. Continue ahead to cross
field and go through woods. Turn L on road, leaving GW. Pass
farm and turn R up gated track. As track gently climbs, the South
Downs come into view in the distance ahead.

Some 250 yards (225 m) after pond on R, look for turn to R, to
go steeply up sandy track through woods. At top, bear L to go
along edge of ridge. At field corner turn R then L to follow path up
through woods and around Hascombe Hillfort *(2)*. Eventually
bear L down main track and ignore L fork. Turn L down lane to
pass The White Horse at Hascombe, rejoining GW. Cross road to
stile and keep ahead. Enter woods and immediately bear R steeply
uphill. Turn R on track and at top of rise turn R on cross-track
then L along cross-track and follow across Holloways Heath.

Turn L down road then R on track and follow along the edge of
Burgate Hanger *(3)*. Continue to go parallel to road and up

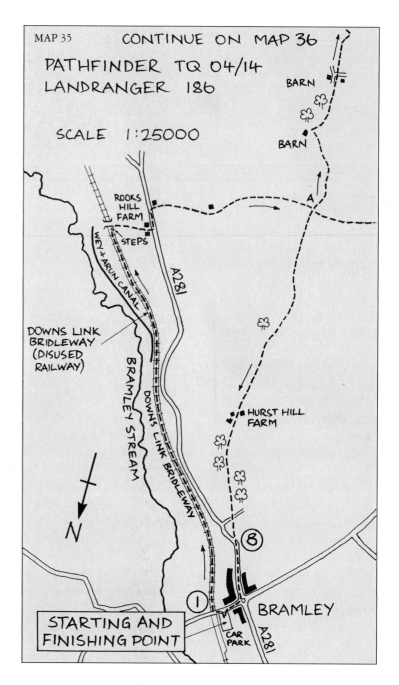

MAP 35   CONTINUE ON MAP 36

PATHFINDER TQ 04/14
LANDRANGER 186

SCALE 1:25000

BARN

BARN

ROOKS
HILL
FARM

STEPS

A281

WEY + ARUN CANAL

DOWNS LINK
BRIDLEWAY
(DISUSED
RAILWAY)

BRAMLEY STREAM

DOWNS LINK BRIDLEWAY

A

HURST HILL
FARM

N

⑧

①

STARTING AND
FINISHING POINT

BRAMLEY

A281

CAR
PARK

through woods. Turn R on track and keep ahead, leaving GW. At wood edge, go up sunken track and ignore track to R to reach summit of Hydon's Ball *(4)*. Go to L of seat then bear R down track. Turn L on wide track, then turn R on cross-track by sandstone pillar and follow to road. Turn R and, at top of rise, turn L on track, then bear L through chestnut coppice. Bear L down track, keep ahead on wide forest track then turn R uphill on cross-track. At T-junction, turn L, go ahead along lane then turn

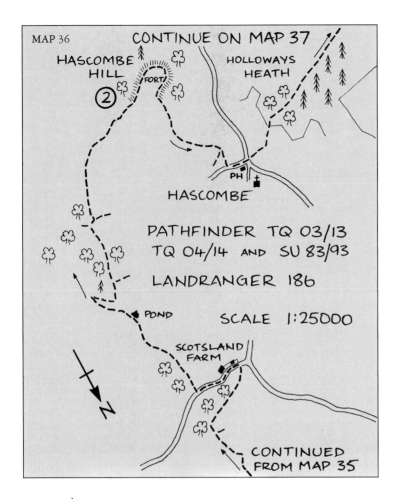

R to road.

Cross road to go through Winkworth Arboretum car-park (5). Pass donation box and go to L of house to pass café (seasonal) and toilets. Bear L down the azalea steps. Keep ahead past lakes and turn L along road. Where road goes R, bear L up drive and in front of cottage, look for, and turn R through, holly arch to go to R of double garage. Follow path ahead over stiles and along field edges to road. Turn R then L on road to Bramley. Immediately before house, turn R up track and climb to top of hill with views in all directions. Keep ahead along wood edge, through trees and along field edge to reach track (A).

Turn L, briefly meeting outward route, then almost immediately L again on track. Keep straight ahead past house, along wood edge, past farm and down through woods. Cross road to go along road then path opposite and continue along pavement through Bramley. At roundabout, turn R along Station Road to car-park.

1 *Downs Link Bridleway and Wey–Arun Canal*
    See page 92.

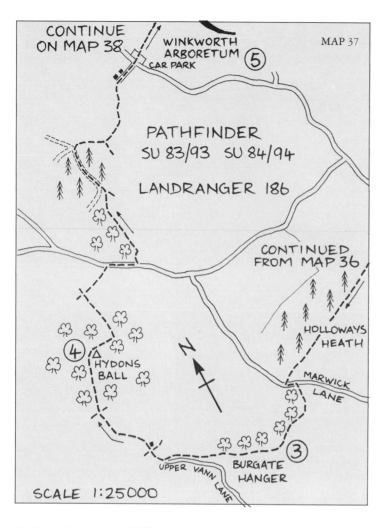

2 Hascombe Iron Age Hillfort

The path runs around the outside of this promontory fort. Like other hillforts along the Greensand ridge it was probably constructed around 200 BC but little is known about the tribe who fortified this site. Many of the mature beech trees which covered the hilltop were uprooted in the 1987 storm.

3 Burgate Hanger

Hanger is a local word for woods clinging to a steep slope. From the path at the foot of the hanger, there are extensive views to the South Downs. Burgate (or Bargate) stone, used for many local buildings, is seen with galleting, chips of ironstone set in the mortar. Like the Rag and Hassock of the eastern Weald, the calcareous Bargate beds give rise to fertile agricultural land.

Autumn, near Hascombe.

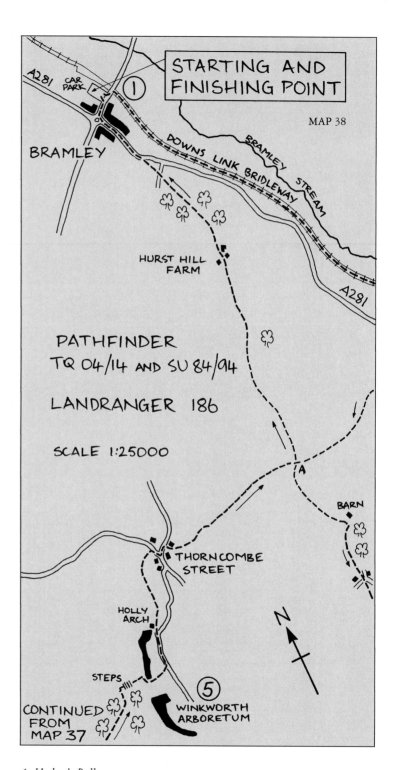

4 Hydon's Ball

The seat on the summit of Hydon's Ball records that this woodland area was given to the NT in 1915 in memory of Octavia Hill, one of the Trust's three co-founders (see page

Maples at Winkworth Arboretum.

172). The sweet chestnut coppice in this area and in nearby woods is being managed in the traditional way.

5   *Winkworth Arboretum*
The Arboretum planted on this sandy hillside has a collection of rare trees and shrubs, and two lakes. It was created out of neglected woodland by Dr Wilfrid Fox, an eminent horticulturalist, between 1938 and 1952 when he donated it to the NT. The route goes straight down the hillside but a detour to visit other parts of the Arboretum in strongly recommended.

3·19

LEITH HILL AND THE HURTWOOD

STARTING AND FINISHING
POINT
Friday Street car-park. Take the
road signed to Leith Hill off the
A25 Guildford–Dorking road to
the west of Wotton and turn first
L to Friday Street
(TQ 04/14–126458). Alternative
car-park for 9 miles (14 km)
circuit lies to north of A (TQ
04/14–108451).
LENGTH
13 miles (21 km). The route can be
divided into two circuits of 6½ and
9 miles (10 and 14 km) by walking
from A to B along the road
through Holmbury St Mary.
ASCENT
2080 ft (634 m)

A very scenic, strenuous, switchback walk across the tree-clad
Greensand hills culminating in Leith Hill, the highest point in
Downs and Weald. In October 1987 the south-facing escarpment
took the brunt of the storm turning this part of the walk into an
assault course. The contrast between the storm damage seen on
the escarpment compared with the more sheltered dip slope is
still striking.

ROUTE DESCRIPTION (Maps 39–42)

From car-park, face road and follow path along R bank. Go down
steps and turn R up track. At five-way junction, bear R. Turn R on
broad cross-track and follow to road at Abinger. Go along path
opposite and cross road to follow enclosed path. Keep ahead
through woods and later go steeply downhill and ahead along
track to road at Holmbury St Mary (A). Turn R along pavement.
Turn L through entrance to Hurtwood Control car-park 9 (1).

Go ahead up track and, at cross-track, turn R steeply uphill and
keep straight ahead. Pass Youth Hostel on R, continue ahead to go
over cross-track and bear R down second track. Follow, ignoring
all paths off to pass fields to R and eventually cross valley bottom
and keep ahead. Just before enclosed path ahead, turn L to go
parallel to boundary on R and over cross-track to road. Go ahead
and down to road. Turn L and then R on track at Gasson Farm.

Bear R on path opposite barn to pass pole on R and go steeply
uphill. Go over cross-track and ahead on broad track to follow
switchback path across the Hurtwood from where the North
Downs can be glimpsed across the Tillingbourne valley to the R.
At T-junction in valley bottom turn R then L to go steeply uphill.
Cross lane and go along track to lane. Continue ahead, then down
track. Go over track and up and then steeply down on path. Go
over track, up path and ahead on track across valley, over cross-
track then, where track bears L, bear R on path down to Wickets
Well (2).

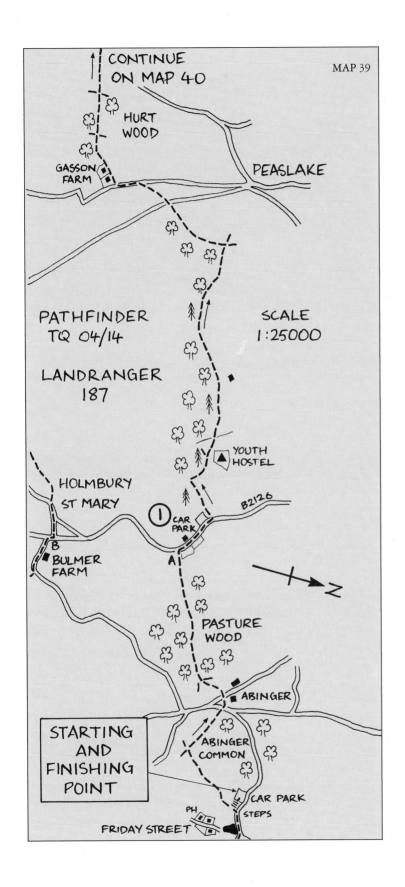

CONTINUE
ON MAP 40

MAP 39

HURT
WOOD

PEASLAKE

GASSON
FARM

PATHFINDER
TQ 04/14

SCALE
1:25000

LANDRANGER
187

YOUTH
HOSTEL

HOLMBURY
ST MARY

B2126

① CAR
PARK

B
BULMER
FARM

A

N

PASTURE
WOOD

ABINGER

STARTING
AND
FINISHING
POINT

ABINGER
COMMON

CAR PARK

STEPS

PH

FRIDAY STREET

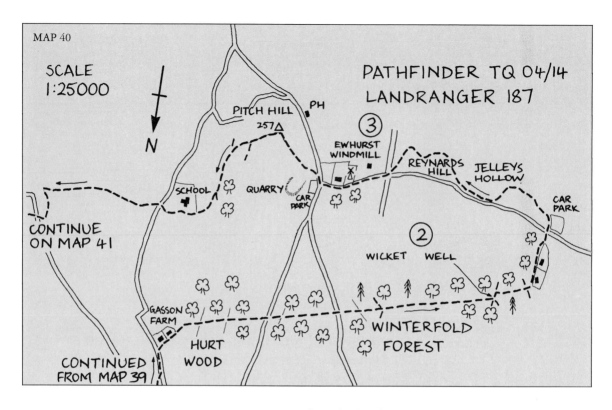

Cross track and take the R of two paths ahead uphill, then down to cross-track to garden hedge. Turn L and keep close to hedge, then field. Bear R on cross-track, then keep ahead to cross road to car-park from where there is the first of many superb views from the greensand ridge across the Weald to the South Downs. At end of parking area, turn L on track to join GW.

Bear R and 330 yards (300 m) later turn L on path, cross drive and keep ahead to road. Turn R past Jelly's Hollow on R then go ahead up path parallel to road. Turn R on path and follow around Reynard's Hill. Near viewpoint, bear L down main track to car-park. Turn R on road, over T-junction and up track opposite. Pass Ewhurst windmill on R *(3)* and bear R down to road. Cross to car-park entrance and almost immediately turn R and follow main path uphill to summit of Pitch Hill.

Keep ahead past OS trig point then turn L on path along edge of hill. Pass seat on R and shortly after, bear R down path. Turn L on track, pass house on L and 300 yards (275 m) later turn R on path. Cross over track and follow path ahead to go along Duke of Kent school drive. Bear L across road and follow fenced path between fields. Bear R on track then turn L up track and bear R to cross road to car-park. Shortly before barrier at end of car-park turn R on path and follow, ignoring all paths off, to go through rampart of Holmbury hillfort to memorial seat on summit *(4)*.

At seat, turn L to follow path around hillside. Eventually merge

Leith Hill tower – the highest point in the Weald.

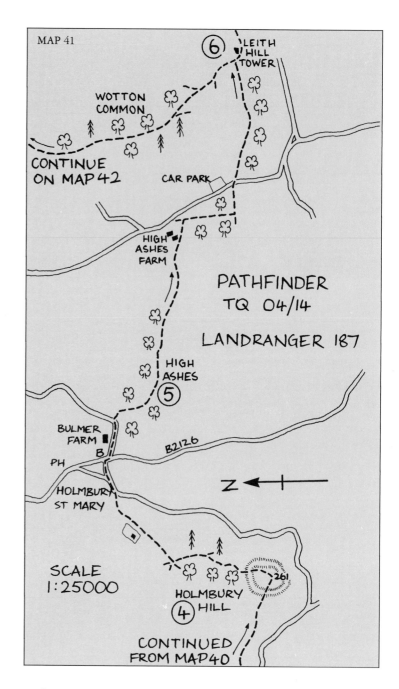

MAP 41

⑥ LEITH HILL TOWER

WOTTON COMMON

CONTINUE ON MAP 42

CAR PARK

HIGH ASHES FARM

PATHFINDER TQ 04/14

LANDRANGER 187

HIGH ASHES ⑤

BULMER FARM
B
PH
B2126

Z

HOLMBURY ST MARY

SCALE 1:25000

261
HOLMBURY ④ HILL

CONTINUED FROM MAP 40

with grassy track and follow to five-path junction. Turn R and follow track to road. Turn L and bear R on road. At T-junction, turn R (B) then turn L on road. Turn R on track opposite white house and follow, going gradually uphill through woods *(5)* to finally pass High Ashes Farm on L. At T-junction, turn R, keep ahead and turn L at next T-junction. Bear R across road and follow track ahead uphill to Leith Hill tower *(6)*.

Just before tower, turn L on track, leaving GW. Bear R down-

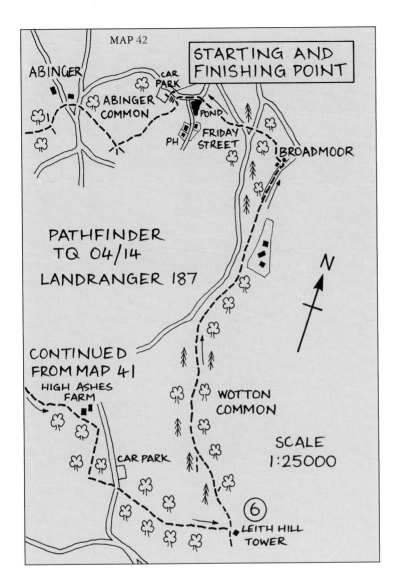

MAP 42

STARTING AND FINISHING POINT

ABINGER

CAR PARK

ABINGER COMMON

POND

PH

FRIDAY STREET

BROADMOOR

PATHFINDER TQ 04/14

LANDRANGER 187

N

CONTINUED FROM MAP 41

HIGH ASHES FARM

WOTTON COMMON

CAR PARK

SCALE 1:25000

⑥

LEITH HILL TOWER

hill then L uphill. At T-junction, turn R down track and later keep ahead down middle path. At U-bend, take R path then bear L downhill off main track and ahead down road at Broadmoor. Just before Leith Cottage, turn L to go up path. At garden corner turn R, then bear L uphill. Cross lane to path opposite. Cross lane and follow path ahead then go downhill to Friday Street. Turn L on road to pass the old mill pond and keep ahead on road, then path to reach car-park.

1 The Hurtwood

The Hurtwood Control Committee, a voluntary organization registered as a charity, administer the public right of access 'for air and exercise' over 4000 acres (1600 hectares) of privately owned, common land. Hurts is the local name for bilberries which grow over the higher sandy hills.

The common land was part of several manors, but the greater part still belongs to Shere Vachery which has been owned by the Bray family since Tudor times. William Bray planted the first Scots pines on the Hurtwood in 1778 at a time when the hills were covered with a mixture of open heath and broadleaf woodland. Since then, commercial planting and the natural spread of pine and birch has, and is, changing the landscape.

2 *Wickets well*

This well, no longer named on current OS maps, is one of several on the dip slope of these hills. Before the advent of mains water, tenants on the Bray estate used the wells for watering cattle and domestic use.

3 *Ewhurst windmill*

This brick and tarred post-mill was built in about 1820, before the growth of the surrounding pines. Its ornamental sweeps, much shorter than the working ones, were put up when it was converted into a private house.

4 *Holmbury hillfort and memorial seat*

The bracken-covered ramparts of the Iron Age hillfort encircling the summit of Holmbury hill are crossed just before reaching the seat. Like Hascombe and other Iron Age hillforts along the Greensand ridge, little is known about the tribe who fortified the site or the use they made of it. The seat, built from local sandstone, was erected in memory of the brothers Reginald and Jocelyn Bray, Lords of the Manor, for their love and work for the Hurtwood 1869–1964.

5 *High Ashes woods*

The beech woods were severely damaged by the 1987 storm. To the right of the track, mossy areas mark a spring line found where the freely draining Hythe beds of the Lower Greensand meet the impervious Atherfield Clay underlying them.

6 *Leith Hill tower*

The tower, now in the ownership of the NT, was built on the highest hill in the Downs and Weald by Richard Hull, a Bristol merchant, in 1764. The battlements and present staircase are later additions and it now houses a small exhibition and tea shop. From its top, 1000 ft (305 m) above sea level, there is a commanding view. When first built on the then heather-clad hills it was a focal point for miles around.

Cobham and The North Kent Downs

STARTING AND FINISHING POINT

Car-park off The Street, Cobham, Kent. Entrance is next to Cobham Primary school (TQ 66/76–671684). Car-park for 7 mile (11.2 km) circuit is at NT Coldrum car-park (TQ 66/76–650607).

LENGTH

16 miles (26 km). The walk can be split into two circuits using link A–C thus: to complete an $8^{1}/_{2}$ mile (14 km) circuit from Cobham at A, go ahead up 'No through road' and turn L up track to broad cross-track at C.

To complete a 7 mile (11 km) circuit, park at the NT Coldrum car-park. Go along path to Coldrum Stones, B. Turn R and follow route description. At C, keep ahead downhill and turn R on road to A. Turn L and follow route description.

ASCENT

2450 ft (750 m)

From the attractive village of Cobham with its many reminders of the time when its fortune was closely linked with the owners of Cobham Hall, the walk traverses the woods and farmland of the undulating northern slopes of the North Kent Downs descending from the escarpment to visit Coldrum Long Barrow. No main roads are crossed and the small settlements passed seem remote from the bustle of the Thames Estuary a few miles to the north.

ROUTE DESCRIPTION (Maps 43–46)

From car-park, turn R along road. Pass The Leather Bottle on R *(1)* then turn L on footpath to pass Cobham church and college on L *(2)*. Keep ahead to go between fields to road. Turn L over railway, then R along field edge in front of house. Cross stile and gate and go downhill across field to houses. Go half L across road to follow footpath up across fields, through wooded strip then downhill towards Luddesdown village hall. Keep ahead up lane, pass Luddesdown and Dode church then turn L over stile in farmyard, joining WW.

Follow fence on L then go alongside hedgerow on R and keep straight ahead to go across field, over stile then diagonally across valley to road. Turn R, ignore 'No through road' (A) and continue ahead along road. When road goes R, keep ahead over stile and follow path through coppice woodland, diagonally across field and along field edge on R. Bear R along fenced track and go ahead over stile to lane. Cross lane and field to road. Turn L, then, when road goes R, go ahead along field edge. In 90 yards (82 m) cross stile and continue in same direction following hedge on R.

Turn R along road and, just before building, turn L to follow path straight ahead through unworked and worked coppice. Go over cross-track and steeply down the scarp slope of the Downs. Turn R at track T-junction, briefly meeting the NDW, and at road turn L down path. From the path, views across the Medway valley open up and the two arms of the North Kent Downs can be seen

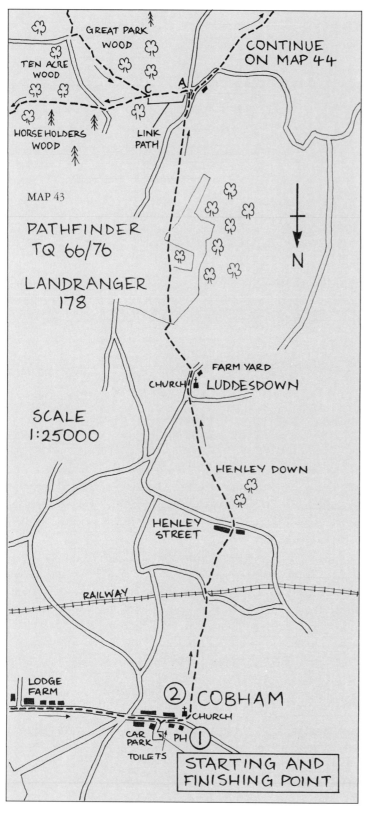

GREAT PARK WOOD

TEN ACRE WOOD

CONTINUE ON MAP 44

HORSE HOLDERS WOOD

C   A

LINK PATH

MAP 43

PATHFINDER TQ 66/76

LANDRANGER 178

N

FARM YARD

CHURCH   LUDDESDOWN

SCALE 1:25000

HENLEY DOWN

HENLEY STREET

RAILWAY

LODGE FARM

② COBHAM
   CHURCH
CAR PARK   PH
TOILETS   ①

STARTING AND FINISHING POINT

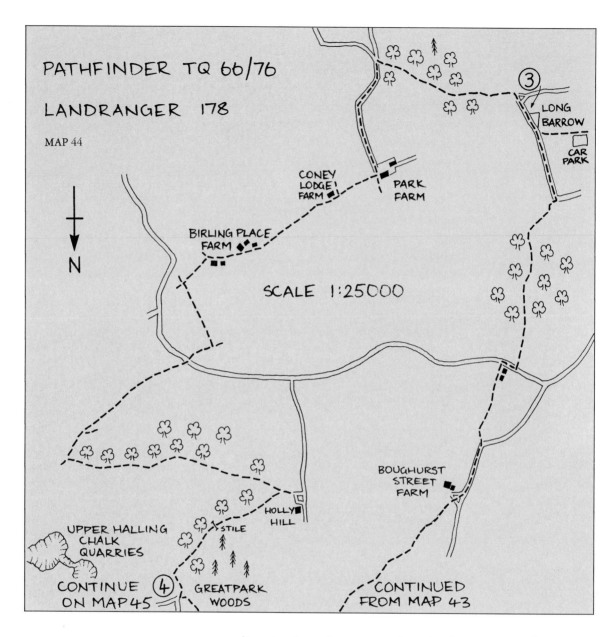

PATHFINDER TQ 66/76

LANDRANGER 178

MAP 44

N

SCALE 1:25000

③ LONG BARROW

CAR PARK

CONEY LODGE FARM

PARK FARM

BIRLING PLACE FARM

BOUGHURST STREET FARM

HOLLY HILL

STILE

UPPER HALLING CHALK QUARRIES

CONTINUE ON MAP 45

④ GREATPARK WOODS

CONTINUED FROM MAP 43

diverging from the gap carved out by the river at Rochester.

Pass Coldrum Long Barrow (B) *(4)*, and follow concrete road. Where this goes R, keep ahead, then turn L at field corner, leaving WW. Follow path across fields and through storm-damaged woods to road. Turn L to Park Farm and turn R along concrete track to pass Coney Lodge and Birling Place Farms. At end of buildings on L, turn L up path across field. In middle of field, turn L on cross-track and at T-junction turn R along track. Go half L across road to continue on track along the foot of the escarpment with chalk quarries of Upper Halling ahead *(5)*.

At lane, turn L for 15 yards (13 m) then turn R to follow path

Previous page: Cauldron long barrow.

along edge of woods and uphill. Cross stile and go along R-side of field. Then, 50 yards (46 m) before field corner, look for and turn R at old metal kissing gate and go across field to line of trees. There are views across Medway valley. Cross stile and follow path through storm-damaged woodland, later going alongside fence on R and along track. By pylon, turn L, then shortly R to follow small path, keeping close to wood edge on R. At pylon in wood turn R and immediately L.

At hilltop, meet cross-track (C) and turn R away from it to meet and follow NDW diagonally across field with the first and only glimpse of the Thames Estuary ahead. At apex of grass triangle, go ahead over track and through woods. Where track goes L, bear R over stile, across field and through woods. Go over cross-track and keep ahead. Go half R across field and into woods. Go over broad cross-track to bear R then turn L. Keep ahead through woods, then just after second overhead cable turn steeply down cross-path. Follow path across field, through woods, down field, along R-side of field and bear L uphill to Upper Bush, passing a fine timber-framed medieval hall house.

Continue down lane, then, where the lane turns L, go straight ahead over field following line of poles, leaving NDW. Turn L on road, then R on track to go under railway, and continue straight ahead uphill across large field (path may be indistinct). As the path climbs, the new housing developments at Cruxton and the outskirts of Rochester come into view to R. Keep woods on L to cross stile in field corner. Go diagonally across field to stile in top L-hand corner (path may be indistinct) and follow path up through the storm-damaged woods of Cobham Park. At top, turn L along wide track.

Pass the neglected Mausoleum *(6)* and follow the main track down through woods and along field edge from where Cobham Hall *(7)* can be seen away to R. Pass Lodge Farm, the old home farm for Cobham Hall. Cross road to go ahead up The Street to car-park.

A scarecrow near Luddesdown. The field is a particularly good example of the thin soil over chalk in this area.

1 The Leather Bottle
This heavily-restored, half-timbered building is the hostelry featured in Charles Dickens' *Pickwick Papers* and a fine collection of Dickensian prints and photographs can be viewed during opening hours.

2 St Mary Magdalene Church and Cobham College
The de Cobham family acquired their lands in Cobham during King John's reign and they and their heirs dominated the village for 400 years. The wide chancel, built by the family in about 1220, houses copies of four tilting helmets (the originals are in the Tower of London), and a magnificent collection of

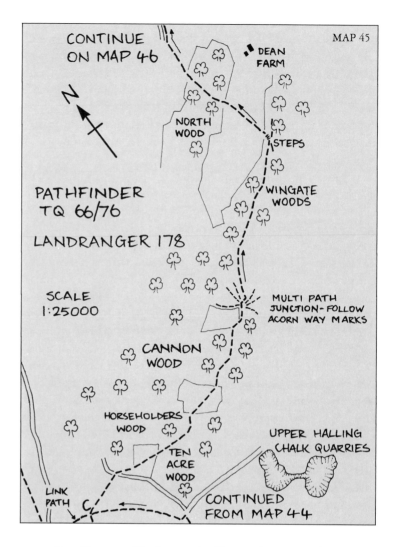

medieval brasses. The brasses had been taken up and neglected before they were relaid in their present position in 1837. Between 1360 and 1370 Sir John de Cobham rebuilt the nave and added the tower and the porch with its parvis, or upper room. He also founded Cobham College behind the church to support a master and four priests who were to say masses for the souls of his ancestors. The College was dissolved, along with the monasteries, in 1537 and was deserted for 50 years before the buildings around the main quadrangle were converted into 20 almshouses. The New College still provides sheltered accommodation for the aged.

4 *Coldrum Long Barrow*

This Neolithic chambered tomb built by some of the first farmers in the area is in the ownership of the NT. When the tomb was opened in 1910, 22 skeletons of both sexes and all ages were discovered, probably all members of a family group. A

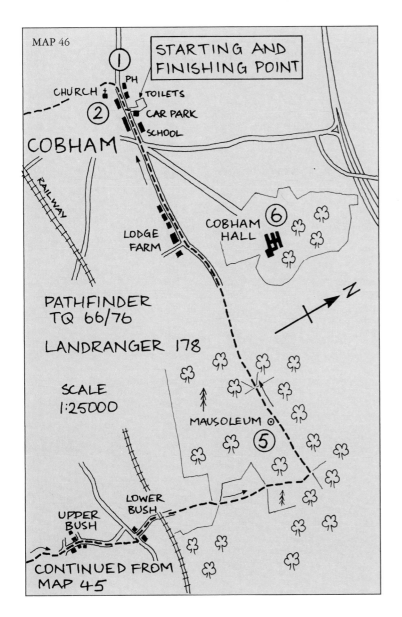

memorial tablet to the Kent prehistorian Benjamin Harrison (1837–1921) wrongly describes it as a stone circle, the confusion resulting from the delapidated state of the now partially restored tomb. Coldrum is one of a small group of chambered tombs in the Medway valley.

5 *Upper Halling Chalk Quarries*
The Downs are dotted with small quarries where chalk has been extracted over the centuries for road materials and for burning in many local lime kilns. During the last century, improved transport and increased demand led to large-scale extraction and, as at Upper Halling, enormous quarries have been cut into the escarpment.

The root ball of a storm damaged beech tree.

6 *Cobham Park Mausoleum*

This forlorn, vandalized Mausoleum, standing on a ridge in the old deer park, was built in the late eighteenth century by the 4th Earl of Darnley, the then owner of Cobham Hall. There are 16 recesses for coffins in the vault of the expensive Portland stone building but strangely it was never consecrated.

7 *Cobham Hall*

The Hall, now a girls' boarding school, was the home of the later de Cobhams and their heirs, and the Darnleys. The brick-built wings date from Elizabethan times and the Hall has been added to throughout the centuries. Until the estate was broken up, the Hall and surrounding park and farmland provided employment for most of the villagers.

3·21

HARTING DOWNS AND THE MARDENS

STARTING AND FINISHING POINT

Harting Downs car-park. From South Harting on B2146 fork L on B2141 and follow signs for viewpoint (SU 61/71−789181).

LENGTH

17 miles (27 km). There is an additional 1½ mile (2.5 km) circuit from A visiting an ancient yew forest.

ASCENT

1650 ft (500 m)

A spectacular Chalk downland walk which visits three delightful churches and the Kingley Vale National Nature Reserve renowned for its great yew forest clinging to the steep slopes of the Downs. A variety of bell, bowl and long barrows have left the indelible stamp of early man on the landscape.

ROUTE DESCRIPTION (Maps 47−49)

From viewpoint in car-park, keep ahead and in 30 yards (27 m) turn R along SDW, with the village of South Harting below and Butser hill behind. Keep ahead to go down and then climb up to Beacon Hill, with the escarpment stretching ahead and the south coast away to the R. The shallow soils show signs of erosion on the steep slopes and the scarp is ploughed just beyond the OS trig point. Go down and up again to top of Pen Hill over several cross-dykes, prehistoric banks and ditches.

Keep ahead and turn R alongside woods. Turn L and then R on track to pass quarry on L. Continue ahead, ignoring R fork. At cross-track detour L and turn L to visit Devil's Jumps (1). Return to route.

Leaving SDW, go ahead over stile, beside fence and then turn R along it to Old Monkton (2). At flint barn, turn R up grass slope to stile and ahead, with superb views over to the spire of Chichester cathedral. At kissing gate, go ahead down through woodland to join track to pass Royal Oak public house. Turn R on track and where it swings R, turn L on grass path. Cross road and go ahead. Turn R along lane and then L to reach North Marden church (3).

Turn R through gate into farmyard and downhill alongside fence. Turn L along field edge and shortly turn R across field over stile. Shortly after stile in field corner, turn L along field margin and at end of field turn L and then R alongside woodland strip. At lane, turn L and then R at T-junction to East Marden.

At next T-junction, turn L past church (4) and at post box turn

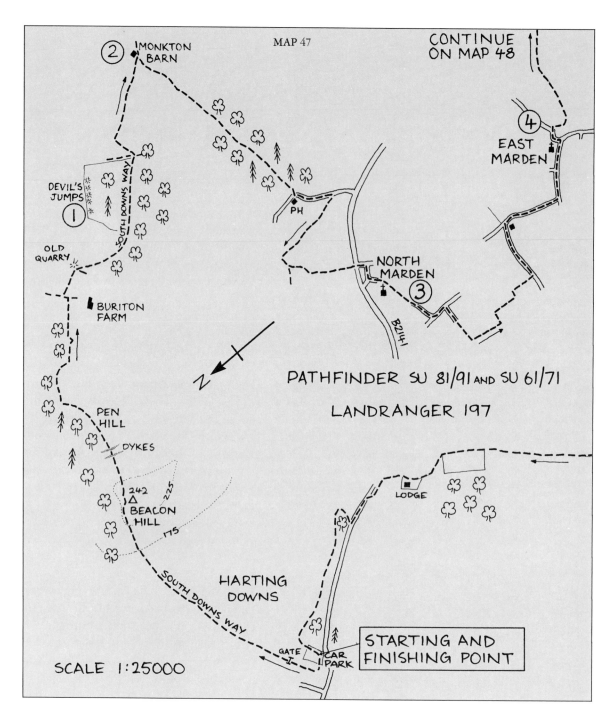

MAP 47

CONTINUE ON MAP 48

② MONKTON BARN

④ EAST MARDEN

DEVIL'S JUMPS ①

SOUTH DOWNS WAY

PH

OLD QUARRY

NORTH MARDEN ③

BURITON FARM

B2141

N

PATHFINDER SU 81/91 AND SU 61/71

LANDRANGER 197

PEN HILL

DYKES

242 △ 225

BEACON HILL

175

LODGE

HARTING DOWNS

SOUTH DOWNS WAY

STARTING AND FINISHING POINT

GATE

CAR PARK

SCALE 1:25000

R up track and then bear L with farm buildings on R. Keep ahead on enclosed track and then go down valley and bear L and then R up to top of steep slope with pines on L. Go ahead along enclosed path towards house. Turn R along track and keep ahead along edge of wood. Where track swings L, bear R on track through woodland. After block of evergreens on L, turn L on cross-path.

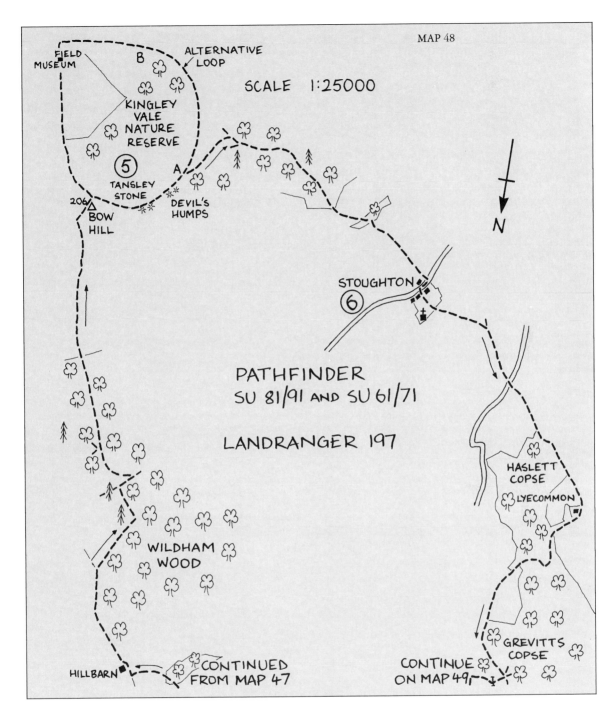

MAP 48

SCALE 1:25000

PATHFINDER
SU 81/91 AND SU 61/71

LANDRANGER 197

Turn R along wide forest track and then turn L at T-junction along hardened forest track. Where track swings L, keep ahead up track and at NCC notice board turn R on cross-track up to Bow Hill and a row of four barrows (5).

For additional loop to visit yew forest, pass barrows on R (A) and fork L downhill, joining Nature Trail at post 22. Follow

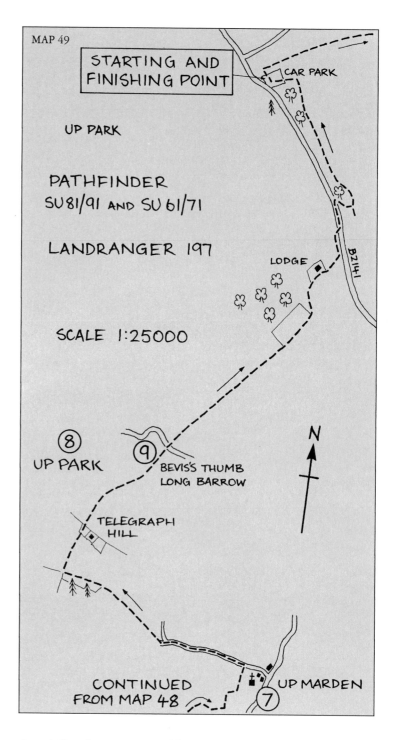

downhill and turn L past Field Museum. Keep ahead and turn R to pass ancient yews. Turn R along fence and turn L steeply up to Tansley Stone. Return to (A).

Keep ahead on track through woods. Turn R along field edge to pass reservoir on L. Continue downhill through woodland to

Stoughton. Turn R along road and then L to church (6). With back to church, turn R through kissing gate and L along field to stile. Turn R up track. Ignore R fork and keep ahead along field edge. Cross lane and go ahead up woodland track. At Lyne Common, bear R with track and keep ahead up enclosed track. Swing R with track and then turn L and ahead along field edge, ignoring R-turn through woodland. Turn R on to cross-path towards field. Cross stile and follow field edge to stile. Turn R to visit Up Marden church (7). Return to route.

Turn L down track and then R on to cross-track to top of Telegraph Hill (8) and down to Bevis's Thumb (9) at road. Cross road and keep ahead on track which joins access drive to road. Just before road, turn L on parallel path and turn L up busy road. In ¼ mile (400 m) turn R and then L on path. Turn L on track and bear L around woods back to car-park.

1 *Devil's Jumps*

This fine row of bell-barrows are prehistoric burial mounds dating from the Bronze Age, 2000–800 BC. Following cremation, the ashes of the dead were placed in pottery vessels and then the mounds were built to mark the spot. Many barrows were plundered by treasure hunters in the nineteenth century and depressions can be seen in the top of these mounds.

2 *Old Monkton*

The remains of a medieval settlement, deserted by the end of the sixteenth century, extends along the floor of this dry valley. Nobody knows why the village was deserted but it may have been as a result of the enclosures when the old-style strip farming was replaced with enclosed fields and many people lost their land. The main trackway along the valley floor linked a series of crofts – terraced platforms on the valley side – and their tofts – their gardens, with adjoining fields. The name Monkton may be associated with the Cistercian monks of Waverley Abbey in Surrey who owned Monkton in the thirteenth century.

3 *North Marden church*

This simple, flint-studded church approached through a farmyard and dedicated to St Mary, is little more than a single room. The population of the parish has always been small and now there are only two services a year – on Good Friday and at Harvest Festival. Its Norman south doorway is worked in Caen stone which was probably shipped across the Channel to Chichester and taken by packhorse to North Marden. The porch shows interesting details of flint flakes set into mortar.

4 *East Marden church*

St Peter's church at East Marden with its weather vane cock-

Arable cultivation and the Weald beyond.

erel perched upon the traditional 'Sussex Cap' spire has a delightful setting surrounded by attractive houses. The Chamber organ within the church belonged to, and was often played by, Prince Albert, Queen Victoria's consort, while it was at St James' Palace. The village well with its thatched roof and square wooden wheel for lowering the bucket lies in front of the church and completes an idyllic picture. There are beehives in the churchyard indicating the importance of churchyards for insects and other wildlife.

5   *Bow Hill and Kingley Vale*

This magnificent row of Bronze Age barrows dominate the skyline. They were built as identical pairs – two bell-barrows, where the flat area surrounded by a ditch resembles the beam of a church bell, and two bowl-barrows which are a traditional pudding shape. All four barrows have been plundered by treasure seekers.

The Kingley Vale National Nature Reserve is renowned for its immense, gnarled yews clinging to the steep-sided coombes cut out of the chalk hillside. The yew is one of three native conifers in Britain and has been growing at Kingley Vale for over 500 years. A few of these ancient yews remain and younger ones have seeded. New trees grow within old and so their girths swell over the centuries. Their massive spread means that light is prevented from reaching the woodland floor and so there is little undergrowth although branches that touch the ground can root and send up new shoots.

The Tansley stone stands as a memorial to Arthur Tansley, the Nature Conservancy Council's first chairman who worked to acquire this reserve in 1952.

6   *Stoughton Church*

The medieval church of St Mary's with its circular graveyard stands on a fine site overlooking the village.

7   *Up Marden church*

The small, remote church of St Michael at Up Marden stands at 500 ft (150 m), surrounded by a farm and cottages. It has always served a small rural community and has changed very little since it was built in the thirteenth century.

8   *Uppark*

The handsome, mellow brick house of Uppark standing on a rise below Telegraph Hill was gutted by fire in August 1989. While many of the treasures were saved, splendid ceilings, chandeliers and carpets were lost.

Now in the ownership of the NT, it was the home of HG

Bronze Age barrows on Bow Hill.

Opposite: North Marden church.

Wells when his mother was the housekeeper and it was offered to Wellington after the battle of Waterloo. He turned it down, reputedly because the drive was so steep, he would have to buy horses for his stables every eighteen months.

9 *Bevis's Thumb*

Bevis's Thumb is a long barrow, an oval burial mound dating from the Neolithic period. The surrounding ditch has been obliterated by both the road and ploughing. In this earlier period, in contrast to the later bell- and bowl-barrows, the bones of the dead were often placed in wooden mortuaries before being covered with earth. Some archaeologists believe that Bevis's Thumb may be connected with the people who dug the causewayed camp on the Trundle.

East Marden church.

3·22

CISSBURY AND CHANCTONBURY RINGS

STARTING AND FINISHING POINT

Small car-park on the west side of the minor road from Sompting to Steyning 1 1/2 miles (2.5 km) north of Sompting which is signed off the A27 Worthing to Shoreham road (TQ 00/10–161080).

LENGTH
19 miles (31 km)

ASCENT
1950 ft (590 m)

Surface flint and chalk near Chanctonbury.

A splendid scenic walk traversing the South Downs and linking two of its most famous landmarks, Cissbury and Chanctonbury Rings. The clump of trees on Chanctonbury Hill make it the most easily recognizable landmark along the Downs and one that can be seen from many different hills in the Downs and Weald.

ROUTE DESCRIPTION (Maps 50–53)

Take the track starting alongside the car-park. Turn L down cross-track, pass flint farm buildings and turn L along concrete track. Where this goes L to road, turn R and follow grassy track up to gate. Turn R to follow grassy path alongside scrub-covered hill-side to eventually go through gate and ahead to NT Cissbury Ring notice. Go half L uphill through scrub (1). When path turns R, go L through gate then R to second gate to reach the ramparts of Cissbury Hillfort (2).

Turn R up steps to follow rampart, passing the OS trig point and the remains of the Neolithic flint mines on L. When rampart starts to swing sharply round to L, bear R down second set of steps, through gate and ahead down field to gate. Follow enclosed path, then turn L at T-junction and follow path past car-park and houses to road. Turn R along pavement then immediately before first bungalow on L, turn L along path. Turn R along cross-path. Bear R along concrete track in front of greenhouses then turn L up rough track. Pass house and lodge and turn R along path from where the church and the eighteenth-century Findon Place come into view. Go alongside flint estate wall on L and turn L on drive to pass the house and church (3).

Immediately past church, bear R through gate and go ahead to stile. Follow grassy path ahead then bear L uphill with hedge. Cross field to stile and go down bank to cross road and go down track opposite. Shortly, turn L on track then L again to follow track as it winds down and then uphill. When track eventually turns L, go ahead through gate and down field, then up track

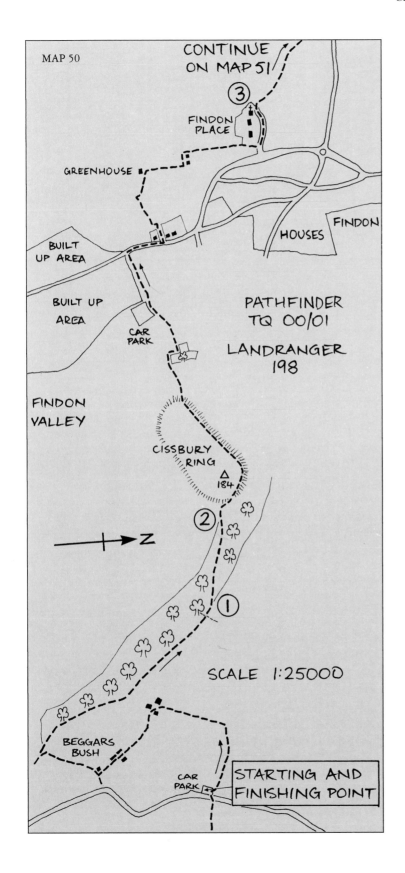

MAP 50

CONTINUE
ON MAP 51

③

FINDON
PLACE

GREENHOUSE

BUILT
UP AREA

FINDON

HOUSES

BUILT UP
AREA

CAR
PARK

PATHFINDER
TQ 00/01

LANDRANGER
198

FINDON
VALLEY

CISSBURY
RING

△
184

②

→ Z

①

SCALE 1:25000

BEGGARS
BUSH

CAR
PARK

STARTING AND
FINISHING POINT

Cissbury ring.

which can be seen ahead. At T-junction, turn L on track then R along lane to Myrtle Grove Farm.

Pass through farm complex with its attractive flint walls and old farm buildings, then, at house ahead, turn L then R on track starting alongside garden. At T-junction, turn R along track. When this bears L by Angmering Park Estate notice, go through gateway on R and bear L along path parallel to line of poles to R. In second field keep going gently uphill with Harrow Hill to the R *(4)* and eventually go through a gate in fence on R, under cables, and ahead downhill to gate. Keep ahead across field to go through gate in far L-hand corner near farm. Turn R through gates then bear L with track and follow it as it winds uphill past arable fields, with Chanctonbury Hill coming into view away to R.

Keep ahead to reach the crest of the South Downs at Chantry Hill *(5)*. Cross track (the SDW), pass car-park and go ahead down road. Where this bears R, turn L on track. Turn R to go past the head of a steep-sided coombe, where, on the unploughed slopes remnants of traditional chalk grassland can be seen. Descend steeply and at bottom bear R through gateway, go ahead through gate and turn L along field edge to pass between brick buildings and ahead along track. At T-junction, turn L on road. Pass a mini-waterfall on R then turn R through gate, pass cottage and turn L through gate to go along field edge. The path runs along a low ridge of Upper Greensand and to the L the Lower Greensand is being dug for building sand. Go through gateway and along drive to pass Sullington Manor and Church *(6)*.

At T-junction, turn R, then L through gate and along field edge bearing R then L at field corner. Bear R to go around farmhouse and keep ahead along track. When this meets lane, turn L, then bear R with lane and keep ahead to cross bridge over the A24 and pass Washington church on L. At T-junction, turn R along road, then turn L over stile opposite road and immediately go half R through gateway and uphill to stile. Follow path up through woods passing a working chalk quarry on R. At T-junction, turn L up track to follow the SDW. Pass old quarries on L and bear L up track. At top, pass the notice describing the dew pond restored by the Society of Sussex Downsmen. Keep ahead past OS trig point to reach Chanctonbury Ring *(7)*.

Continue along track from where there is an excellent view of Cissbury Ring to the R and later along the escarpment of the South Downs beyond with the Adur valley ahead. Keep ahead alongside fence on L and follow track as it passes new pasture and arable fields and gradually bears round to R to eventually meet

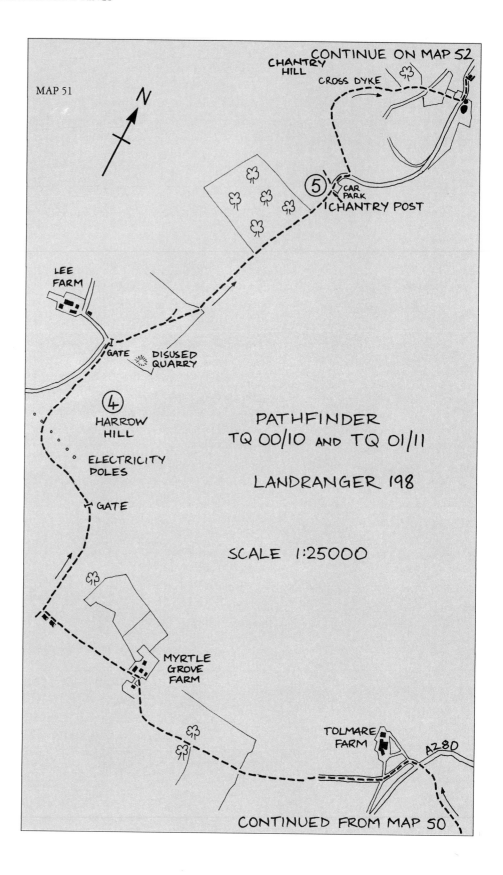

MAP 51

CONTINUE ON MAP 52

CHANTRY HILL

CROSS DYKE

⑤ CAR PARK

CHANTRY POST

LEE FARM

GATE

DISUSED QUARRY

④ HARROW HILL

ELECTRICITY POLES

GATE

PATHFINDER
TQ 00/10 AND TQ 01/11

LANDRANGER 198

SCALE 1:25000

MYRTLE GROVE FARM

TOLMARE FARM

A280

CONTINUED FROM MAP 50

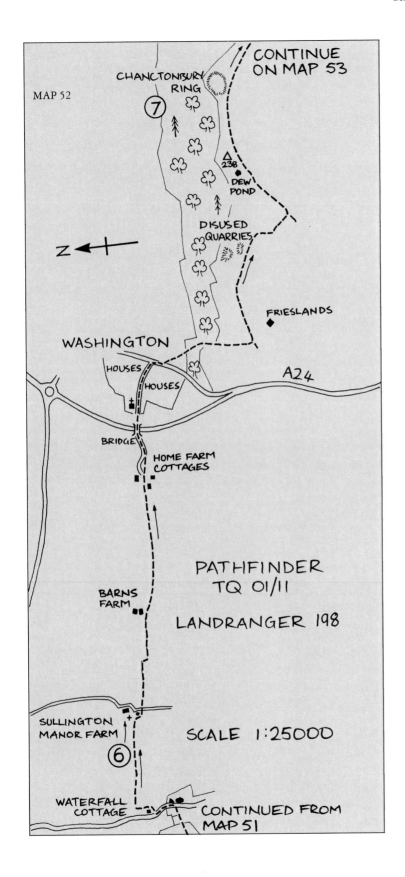

MAP 52

CONTINUE
ON MAP 53

CHANCTONBURY
RING

⑦

238

DEW
POND

DISUSED
QUARRIES

Z

FRIESLANDS

WASHINGTON

HOUSES

HOUSES

A24

BRIDGE

HOME FARM
COTTAGES

PATHFINDER
TQ 01/11

LANDRANGER 198

BARNS
FARM

SULLINGTON
MANOR FARM

⑥

SCALE 1:25000

WATERFALL
COTTAGE

CONTINUED FROM
MAP 51

road. Keep ahead along road passing the dry valley of Steyning Bowl on L. When road turns R, shortly after SDW turns L over stile, go ahead through gate and alongside fence on L. From the path, the Gothic pinnacles of Lancing College can be seen to the L ahead. Turn R on cross-track and follow to road and car-park.

1 *Chalk scrub*
On the steep slope on this side of Cissbury Hill there is a dense growth of scrub with a mixture of bushes and young trees including hawthorn, blackthorn, privet and wayfaring tree, all characteristic of the Downs.

2 *Cissbury Hillfort and Flint Mines*
Over 5000 years ago there was a change from the hunter-gathering way of life, to farming. The Neolithic people who settled in this area dug over 200 flint mines around the hilltop to extract the raw material for their tools and weapons. The mines can be seen as large depressions. Using antler picks and shovels made from the shoulder blades of domestic animals or deer, a vertical shaft was sunk and working galleries opened out from its base. The mines were abandoned during the Bronze Age, then, *c*.300 BC, the impressive Iron Age defences were dug enclosing 60 acres (24 hectares) of the hilltop.

3 *Findon Church*
The flint-clad church is separated from its village by the busy A24. It is a complex building and its roof spanning both the nave and the large northern aisle is most unusual.

4 *Harrow Hill flint mines*
Over 160 flint mines, contemporary with those on Cissbury Hill, have been identified around the hilltop.

5 *Chantry Hill*
As the route climbs to the crest of the Downs at Chantry Hill, many acres of cereals are seen growing on the thin chalky soils. There is a dearth of traditional chalk grassland here and new pasture sown after intensive arable farming bears no relationship to this grassland.

6 *Sullington Manor and Church*
The church has Saxon origins and, together with the manor house, whose occupants were its chief parishioners for many centuries, seems detached from the bustle of twentieth-century life.

7 *Chanctonbury Ring*
There is both a small Iron Age hillfort and the foundations of two Roman buildings at Chanctonbury Ring but it is the clump of beech trees, the first of which were planted within the fort in 1760, that have long provided the traveller with a distant landmark which has made the hill so famous.

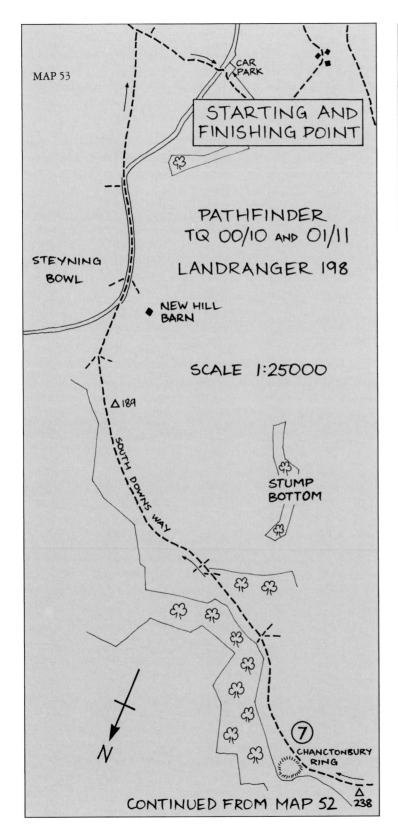

MAP 53

CAR PARK

STARTING AND
FINISHING POINT

PATHFINDER
TQ 00/10 AND 01/11

LANDRANGER 198

STEYNING
BOWL

◆ NEW HILL
BARN

SCALE 1:25000

△ 189

SOUTH DOWNS WAY

STUMP
BOTTOM

⑦

CHANCTONBURY
RING

△ 238

N

CONTINUED FROM MAP 52

The wide expanse of the South Downs near Cissbury.

4·23

BLACKDOWN AND THE DEVIL'S PUNCHBOWL

STARTING AND FINISHING POINT
Waggoners Wells NT car-park signed off the south side of the B3002, Grayshott to Headley Down road (su 83/93–863343).
LENGTH
21 miles (34 km)
ASCENT
2250 ft (690 m)

A splendid scenic walk over the Greensand hills of the western Weald, linking the extensive, tree-clad commons around Haslemere and visiting Blackdown, the second highest point in the Downs and Weald. It is especially recommended in late autumn when the bracken and birch leaves have turned. Most of the route is along dry, sandy tracks but where the clay is crossed to visit the western outposts of the old Wealden iron industry, mud can be expected after a wet spell.

ROUTE DESCRIPTION (Maps 54–57)

Go through car-park entrance at Waggoners Wells *(1)* and where lane turns L, go ahead over footbridge. In 40 yards (37 m) turn L by large fir tree and follow path to go up valley past ponds on L. At houses, turn L steeply up cross-track and at T-junction turn L along road then R along Beech Hanger Road. Turn R with road, then L on rough road. Keep ahead to bear L with track then turn R on path steeply down through trees. Turn L down road, Whitmoor Vale.

Cross stream by Hampshire sign and immediately turn R up small path. Turn R on cross-track to go uphill through trees. 30 yards (27 m) before boundary bank ahead turn R on path – a NT bridleway. At fence corner on L, turn L and follow main track ahead to eventually reach road. Turn L then R on track next to Lloyds Bank training centre. Keep ahead over path junction at Hycombe NT sign then 25 yards (23 m) later, go half R steeply down path. Turn L along track and R through barriers on second path on R to cross two footbridges over the stream at the bottom of the Devil's Punchbowl *(2)*.

Continue ahead uphill to pass a springline on L and Hindhead Youth Hostel on R. Turn L to follow main track along the lower slopes of the Punchbowl ignoring all paths off. Finally, at field corner, keep ahead and turn R up cross-track to join the GW. Follow track, the old Portsmouth Road, to go along the rim of the

166

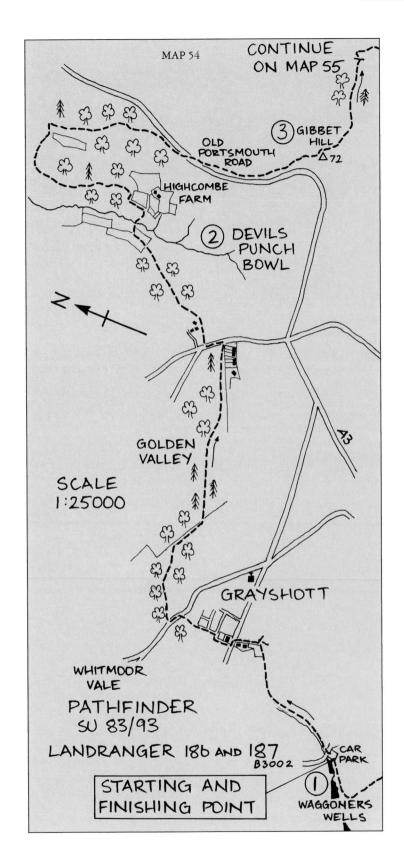

MAP 54

CONTINUE ON MAP 55

③ GIBBET HILL
△ 72

OLD PORTSMOUTH ROAD

HIGHCOMBE FARM

② DEVILS PUNCH BOWL

N

A3

GOLDEN VALLEY

SCALE 1:25000

GRAYSHOTT

WHITMOOR VALE

PATHFINDER SU 83/93

LANDRANGER 186 AND 187
B3002

CAR PARK

① WAGGONERS WELLS

STARTING AND FINISHING POINT

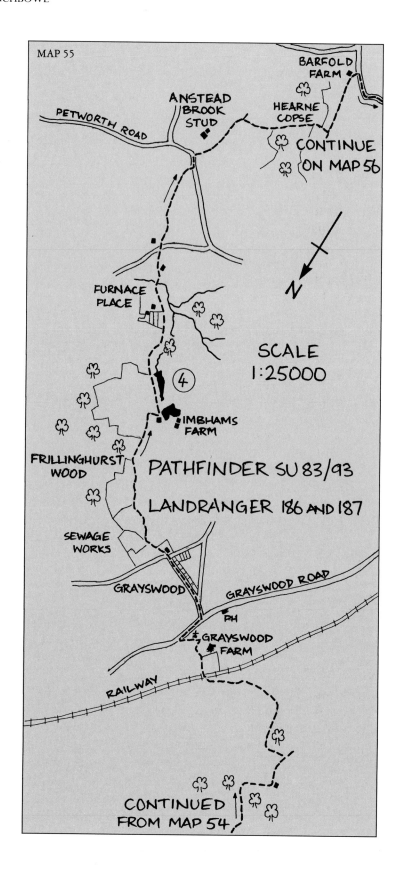

Punchbowl where the heather-covered slopes give some impression of what this old heathland must once have looked like. Bear R across A3 to continue along the old road. Eventually bear L on track, then turn R on cross-path up to cross on Gibbet Hill *(3)*.

From cross, bear L to OS trig point with its viewfinder from where the sweep of the Lower Greensand hills to Leith Hill, the highest point in the Downs and Weald, can be seen. Pass to L of OS trig point, leaving GW, to take small path ahead downhill. Keep ahead over five-track junction, past Hurt Hill NT sign and along ridge to Chalmers memorial seat. Turn L downhill on winding track, ignore all paths off to L then, at NT sign, keep ahead on track to pass house on R. Bear L down broad track. At triangle, turn R to pass under railway to reach road at Grayswood.

Turn R, then L along Lower Road. Keep L, then at end cross Prestwick Lane to go up track opposite. At end go half R across field (path may be indistinct) to go through centre of woodland strip. Bear L across field to stile and gate at field corner. Go along path, straight ahead across field, through gate and turn R along field edge. Turn L along drive and where this swings R go ahead on track. Imbhams' boring-mill pond *(4)*, now used for fishing, can shortly be seen through trees to the R. Continue along drive, then lane, to pass Furnace Court on L. Bear R with lane which runs along the pond bay of a now dry pond. This provided power for the former Imbhams' blast furnace.

Pass house on R and immediately bear R up steps, over stile and ahead over field to stile. Cross road to lane opposite, then, just before garden, turn R to go along field edge on R. Swing L round field corner and turn R through gap opposite cottage. Cross road to go along drive opposite to Anstead Brook Stud. Keep ahead on track. In 300 yards (275 m), just past field corner on L, turn R to go through gate, alongside hedge on R and up through wood to gate. Keep alongside trees on L then go straight across field to turn L along track. Follow to Barfold Farm.

Turn R up road and when this turns R, go ahead up track to R of Blackdown NT sign. Turn L along track. Bear L then keep straight ahead on main track ignoring all paths off to go along the wooded spur of Blackdown. When track eventually swings R, keep ahead on path down through barriers to viewfinder and seat, the Temple of the Winds, for a magnificent view *(5)*.

Retrace steps to track and bear L to continue along it, ignoring all paths off. Cross open area and re-enter woods. Turn L along broad cross-track, ignore track to R and go over a further cross-track before shortly forking L. At T-junction, turn R along path. Go through gate then soon turn R to go across field. Go through gate and bear L downhill to turn L through gate. Turn R along drive, pass Valewood Farmhouse, a delightful tile-hung and sand-

Autumnal bilberry, ling and bracken.

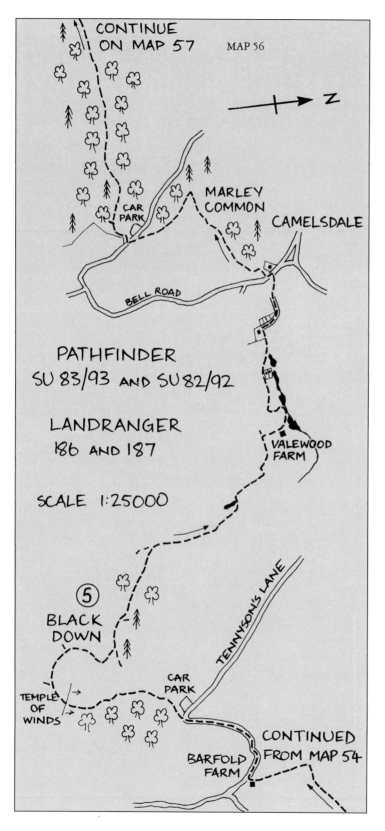

CONTINUE ON MAP 57 MAP 56

N

MARLEY COMMON

CAMELSDALE

CAR PARK

BELL ROAD

PATHFINDER
SU 83/93 AND SU 82/92

LANDRANGER
186 AND 187

SCALE 1:25000

VALEWOOD FARM

⑤
BLACK DOWN

TENNYSON'S LANE

TEMPLE OF WINDS

CAR PARK

CONTINUED FROM MAP 54

BARFOLD FARM

stone building. Go through gateway and immediately turn L on path.

At end of enclosed path, turn R to go uphill alongside old fence on R. Turn R at T-junction and keep ahead along track. Pass brick gateway and at T-junction turn R to pass old mill pond on R. Turn L along lane, pass Lowder Mill on L, and at end turn L and shortly R to cross road and go up track past the Little Sussex Bell. Follow track going L, then R, uphill through Marley Wood. At five-path junction turn L and keep L along track. Cross drive and continue ahead to road. Turn R along road, then just before NT car-park turn L down path. The view from the car-park is worth a short detour.

Look for, and turn R down, path. Turn R to follow path over pond outlet, then bear L with path and follow past old chestnut coppice. Bear L to keep along main track. Just before road, turn R up path. Turn L on cross-path, briefly joining the SBP. Bear L along road, turn L at T-junction and shortly turn R on path by Lynchmere Green. Follow along field edge and through woods. Bear R on main track with worked chestnut coppice on L, and keep R alongside old boundary bank. At field corner keep ahead and at next field corner bear L on path. At five-path junction, meet SBP and go half R up path. Bear R across road to follow path, then drive. At East Lodge turn L down fenced track. Turn R on path parallel to railway. Go through gate and along field edge. Turn L down lane, through farmyard and gate and over railway to reach road by Prince of Wales public house.

Turn R along road and at end of buildings turn L to go steeply up path. At top, bear R along broad track and follow power lines. In 300 yards (275 m) bear L on path alongside boundary bank on L. Turn L on road, then cross A3 via gap in central reservation to go down steps and follow path ahead over Bramshott Common. At T-junction, turn L and just before cross-track turn R down stony track. Ignore all paths off and bear R alongside Waggoners Wells ponds to reach car-park on R.

1 Waggoners Wells

The NT acquired Waggoners Wells in 1919 as a memorial to Sir Robert Hunter (1844–1913), one of the Trusts three co-founders and chairman from its foundation in 1895 until his death. He drew up the Articles of Association and it was his influence that led to the early acquisition of much of the NT's land around Hindhead. At the time of his death, the NT owned 65 properties, including several in the Lake District and Kent, the homes of the other two co-founders Canon Rawnsley and Octavia Hill (see page 66).

The ponds at Waggoners or Wakeners Wells, to give it its

Previous page: The Devil's Punchbowl.

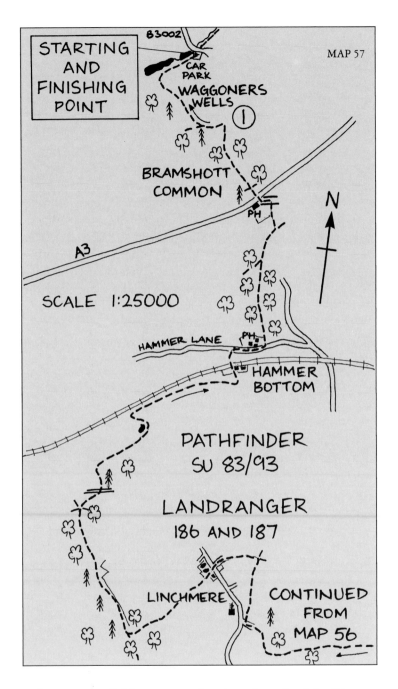

early name, are fed by a stream forming a branch of the River Wey. The origin of the ponds is obscure. The stream may have been dammed to form fish ponds or they could be old hammer ponds for an iron foundry. The middle pond is now used for trout and coarse fishing. With the help of volunteers the NT has restored the causeways and dug out the ponds.

2 The Devil's Punchbowl

Over the centuries, this deep valley formed where springs

Waggoner's Wells.

welling up at their junction with the underlying Atherfield Clay undermined and eroded the sandy Hythe beds of the Lower Greensand. It is part of the 1300 acres (526 hectares) of Hindhead Commons owned by the NT. Birch, pine and bracken have increased over recent years to the detriment of the heath.

3 Gibbet Hill

At 892 ft (272 m) this is Surrey's second highest point. The Victorian cross marks the spot where, in 1786, a sailor's three murderers were hanged. This murder, surely not the only one to have been committed along the old Portsmouth Road, caught Charles Dickens' imagination. Nicholas Nickleby, accompanied by Smyke, read the inscription on a stone erected on the rim of the Devil's Punchbowl and Dickens describes how, 'the blood of the murdered man had run down drop by drop into the hollow which gives the place its name. Devil's Bowl thought Nicholas as he looked into the void never held fitter liquor than that.'

4 The Wealden iron industry and Imbhams' furnace

Iron-rich seams of Wealden clay have been quarried since the Iron Age. Fragmentary remains of Roman bloomeries are concentrated in the eastern Weald which was also the centre for the medieval industry. The first English blast furnace was built at Newbridge on the edge of the Ashdown Forest in 1496. This technological development, imported from the continent, heralded the expansion of the Wealdon iron industry in response to an increasing military demand for canons, and wrought iron for the domestic market. Around 4000 acres (1619 hectares) of coppice was needed to provide a renewable supply of fuel for each furnace and its forge and the industry spread into the woodlands of the western Weald. Imbhams' blast furnace, one of several around Haslemere, was built about 1574 and by 1664 a boring-mill for casting guns had been built near the present Furnace House. It was unable to cope with competition from the developing coal-based industries in the Midlands and Scotland and soon fell into disuse.

5 Blackdown

The distinctive long ridge of Blackdown, the second highest point in the Downs and Weald, can be seen from many viewpoints. Trees, predominantly Scots pine, now cover much of this common land but where open heathland remains, bilberries grow among the heather and spreading bracken. The OS trig point is hidden in the trees but from the viewpoint there is a magnificent panorama across the Low Weald to the Ashdown Forest, Ditchling Beacon and Chanctonbury Ring, all visited on other routes in this book.

Beachy Head and Lullington Heath

STARTING AND FINISHING POINT

Forestry Commission car-park on the A259 west of Friston Forest (TV 49/59/69–515003). There is an alternative car-park at Jevington (TV 49/59/69–562013).

LENGTH

27 miles (43 km). This walk can be split into two circuits thus: One is 14 miles (23 km) long. Follow the route description from A to B. The second is 20 miles (32 km) long. Follow the route description from C to D. From D, the SDW provides an alternative route back to the car-park.

ASCENT

2700ft (820 m)

SHORTER ROUTES

A–B: Short circuit back to car-park from Jevington on 14 mile (23 km) loop. At A turn L along road and R at 'P' sign. Follow track uphill. At top of slope, go ahead on forest track, over stoney cross-track. Keep ahead to join route description from B.

C–D: Short circuit back to car-park from Alfriston on 20 mile (32 km) loop. Just before second footbridge, turn L over stile along the Cuckmere river. Just before white bridge, turn L on tarmac path and turn L along road. Turn R up farm access track and continue from D in route description.

This very strenuous walk with breathtaking views of sea and Chalk downland visits the grandest coastal scenery in the Downs and Weald. From the mouth of the river Cuckmere, the Seven Sisters stretch up to Beachy Head which, at 530 ft (168 m), is the highest Chalk sea cliff in Great Britain. The soft chalk of these dramatic cliffs is continually eroding and walkers should on no account go close to the cliff edge.

The walk visits several attractive villages and the tiny church at Lullington set high on the Downs overlooking Alfriston within the quiet valley of the river Cuckmere. From the lofty Firle Beacon, one of the highest points on the South Downs, the walk returns through Lullington Heath National Nature Reserve which is renowned for its chalk heathland. During dry weather, fire is a serious threat to the heathland. Please take care not to start fires or drop matches.

ROUTE DESCRIPTION (Maps 58–65)

From car-park entrance, turn L down the road. Ignore L turn to West Dean and church and where road bends R, go ahead up track, through gate and later bear R along track. At road turn L entrance to Seven Sisters Country Park car-park (1) go ahead through gate on wide, grassy track along the flood plain of the River Cuckmere, joining SDW. Keep ahead down concrete track and where it bends L go ahead through gate. Soon bear L on track and later go through gate by pillbox and then turn L steeply uphill. Ahead stretch the Seven Sisters (2) and, behind, a bird's eye view of the River Cuckmere. Eventually, after a superb cliff top walk, turn R and then L along stoney track into Birling Gap.

Keep ahead across road and up steps to viewpoint at Belle Tout lighthouse and continue along cliffs to Beachy Head. Just before café and car-park, detour L to visit the Countryside Centre in the old Signalman's Cottage (2). Return to route. Keep ahead down verge parallel to road. Eastbourne can be seen ahead. At T-junc-

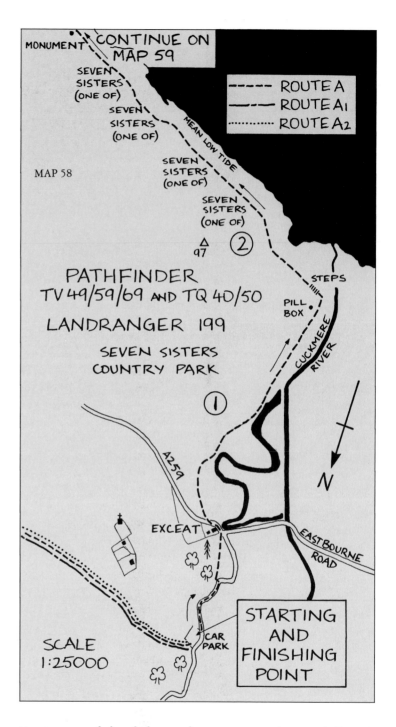

MAP 58

CONTINUE ON MAP 59

MONUMENT

SEVEN SISTERS (ONE OF)

SEVEN SISTERS (ONE OF)

MEAN LOW TIDE

ROUTE A
ROUTE A1
ROUTE A2

SEVEN SISTERS (ONE OF)

SEVEN SISTERS (ONE OF)

△ 97

②

PATHFINDER
TV 49/59/69 AND TQ 40/50

LANDRANGER 199

SEVEN SISTERS
COUNTRY PARK

STEPS

PILL BOX

CUCKMERE RIVER

①

A259

N

EXCEAT

EASTBOURNE ROAD

STARTING
AND
FINISHING
POINT

CAR PARK

SCALE
1:25000

tion turn L and shortly bear R down grassy track towards Jevington *(3)* passing dew ponds on R. Cross road and keep ahead across golf course. Eventually, leaving SDW, go downhill on tree-lined track, and bear R over stile and down across field to L of house and keep ahead to Jevington.

At T-junction (A), turn R along road, and detour L to visit

church. Turn L just before 'Coopers' and bear R beside house to go ahead under cables and across field to stile. Keep ahead to turn R on track and then bear L up path. Turn R along field edge and then ahead across field to L of building. Keep ahead, and then bear R on track and immediately L up path. Bear R over grassy area, go over stile and then down and around hillside. Go down to another stile and ahead to track (path may be indistinct). Turn L along track joining WW. Detour R to visit St Peter's Church, Folkington *(4)*. Return to route.

Keep ahead up track, ignore first gate on L and then bear L up through gate and continue over open Down with views ahead to Firle Beacon. Keep ahead, passing under Long Man *(4)* on L with views down to village of Wilmington. Go over cross-track, leaving WW, and then turn L and R around reservoir fence. Cross road to go along track to R of parking area. Leaving SDW, turn L over stile and go half R across fields and look for stile on L. To visit Lullington church *(4)*, turn L along field edge and then bear L.

Turn R down stepped path to road. Go diagonally ahead to cross two footbridges into Alfriston (C), rejoining SDW. To visit church and NT Clergy House *(5)*, bear L and return to route. Go ahead up enclosed path. Turn R along street and then L beside Star Inn. Keep ahead over road up King's Ride and then ahead up track. Where track swings L, keep ahead, and follow to top of Bostal Hill to reach car-park on R. To visit Firle Beacon, keep ahead uphill to OS trig point *(6)*. Return to route.

Turn L past farm buildings, leaving SDW, and keep ahead on track. Eventually, at multi-path junction, fork L and keep ahead on track. At field, bear L along field edge and keep ahead on track. Turn R through gate, go diagonally across road and turn L on path parallel to road and then continue along road. Bear R over stile and then bear L. Go over stream to cross stile and ahead down raised bank to footbridge. Turn L and follow tarmac path to road at Litlington. Turn L along road and then turn R (D) and L past farm buildings. Follow track up to Lullington Heath National Nature Reserve *(7)*; with fine views down into Deepdene and an interesting dew pond off path to L. Continue ahead down into dip and turn R over stile. Keep ahead through the reserve to Charleston Bottom. Eventually, at multi-path junction in valley bottom, go ahead up stoney track to Snag Hill. Ignore track on L to Jevington and forest ride on R to go steeply uphill and turn R on to cross-track (B). Where forest track swings L, go ahead on grassy track and through gate. Continue along forest ride and fork R on track waymarked forest walk. Go over broad cross-track and turn L down track and then R joining SDW. Ignore track L and turn L parallel with overhead cables. Turn R under cables and fork L down forest walk and back to car-park.

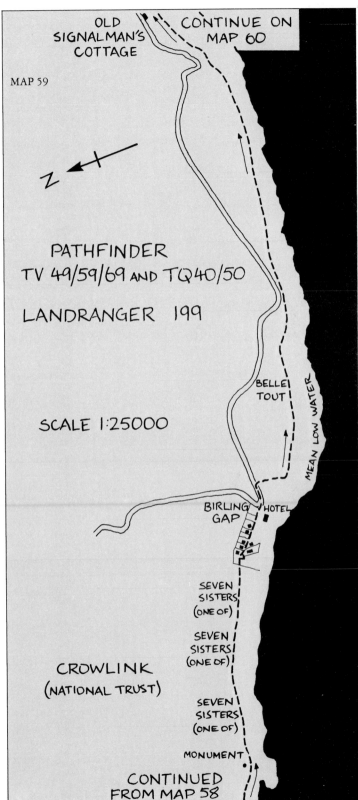

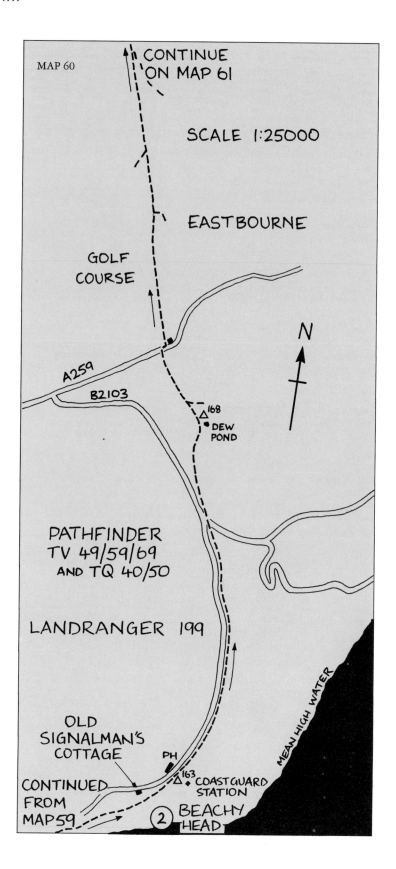

MAP 60

CONTINUE ON MAP 61

SCALE 1:25000

EASTBOURNE

GOLF COURSE

N

A259

B2103

△168 ● DEW POND

PATHFINDER TV 49/59/69 AND TQ 40/50

LANDRANGER 199

MEAN HIGH WATER

OLD SIGNALMAN'S COTTAGE

PH

CONTINUED FROM MAP 59

△163 ● COASTGUARD STATION

② BEACHY HEAD

Previous page: *The Seven Sisters.*

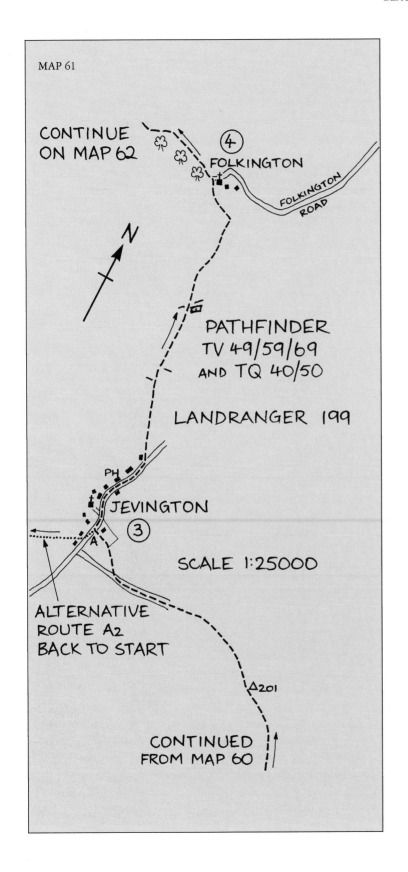

MAP 61

CONTINUE
ON MAP 62

④ FOLKINGTON

FOLKINGTON ROAD

N

PATHFINDER
TV 49/59/69
AND TQ 40/50

LANDRANGER 199

PH

JEVINGTON

③

A

SCALE 1:25000

ALTERNATIVE
ROUTE A2
BACK TO START

A201

CONTINUED
FROM MAP 60

1 Seven Sisters Country Park

The serpentine Cuckmere river winds its way to the sea through placid water meadows and saltings. It is the only river between Dover and Southampton without a port at its head. Although its mouth is now blocked with shingle, it was once a smugglers' route with wool being exchanged for brandy, silk and tea. The Seven Sisters Country Park opened in 1971 when this part of the Cuckmere valley was bought by East Sussex County Council. The Park Centre in an eighteenth-century barn is well worth a visit.

2 Seven Sisters and Beachy Head

From the mouth of the Cuckmere to Birling Gap, the dry valleys between the Seven Sisters hang high above the sea. From the Gap the cliffs rise again to Beachy Head. They are continually battered by waves and often fall in great blocks with the areas of cliff between forming miniature headlands.

The attractive Belle Tout lighthouse was built in 1831 but was replaced by the present red and white lighthouse at the foot of the cliff in 1902. On a clear day, the Royal Sovereign light tower can be seen from 8 miles (13 km) out to sea.

The Signalman's Cottage was built in 1898 to house employees of Lloyds of London who observed and signalled to passing ships. It has now been converted into a Countryside Centre by Sussex Wildlife Trust.

3 Jevington

This unspoilt flint and brick village is set in a small, dry valley. The church, with its massive tower, stands on a knoll and is dedicated to St Andrew the fisherman whose diagonal stone cross can be seen on the church roof. The unusual anchor crosses also symbolize its seafaring connections. A Saxon sculpture was discovered in the church in 1875 when the belfry was refloored.

4 Folkington Church, Long Man of Wilmington and Lullington Church

The small church at Folkington nestling under the Downs is built of stone, faced with flint and serves a few scattered houses. To the west lies the Long Man of Wilmington: an immense chalk figure 230 ft (70 m) high, marked out with 700 white concrete blocks on Windover Hill. He overlooks the village of Wilmington and the remains of the Wilmington Priory. With arms outstretched skywards and a staff in each hand some say that he is the Wilmington giant slain in battle after a quarrel with another giant living over at Firle Beacon.

To the west, set high upon the Downs, lies the tiny church of Lullington. Seating a congregation of only 20 people, it is now one of the smallest churches in the country although it was once the chancel of a much larger one.

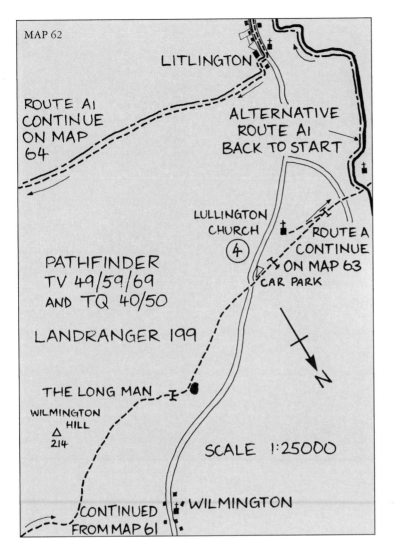

MAP 62

LITLINGTON

ROUTE A1
CONTINUE
ON MAP
64

ALTERNATIVE
ROUTE A1
BACK TO START

LULLINGTON
CHURCH
④

ROUTE A
CONTINUE
ON MAP 63

CAR PARK

PATHFINDER
TV 49/59/69
AND TQ 40/50

LANDRANGER 199

N

THE LONG MAN

WILMINGTON
HILL
△
214

SCALE 1:25000

CONTINUED
FROM MAP 61

WILMINGTON

Alfriston.

5 *Alfriston and the Clergy House*

The pretty Downland village of Alfriston lies in the heart of the Cuckmere valley. It stands on the site of an old Saxon settlement and in the late twelfth century was granted a charter by Richard I to hold a market. The market cross in Waterloo Square was a symbol to remind traders to deal honestly with customers. Alfriston was a port until 1732 and barges used to bring goods to the village until 1915, but now the mouth of the Cuckmere is blocked by shingle.

Alfriston's magnificent church, known as the 'Cathedral of the Downs', stands on a mound beside the village green known as the Tye. One of the very few medieval clergy houses to survive stands adjacent to the church. Shortly after the foundation of the NT in 1895 (see page 172), it was bought for ten pounds and was the first building to be acquired by the Trust.

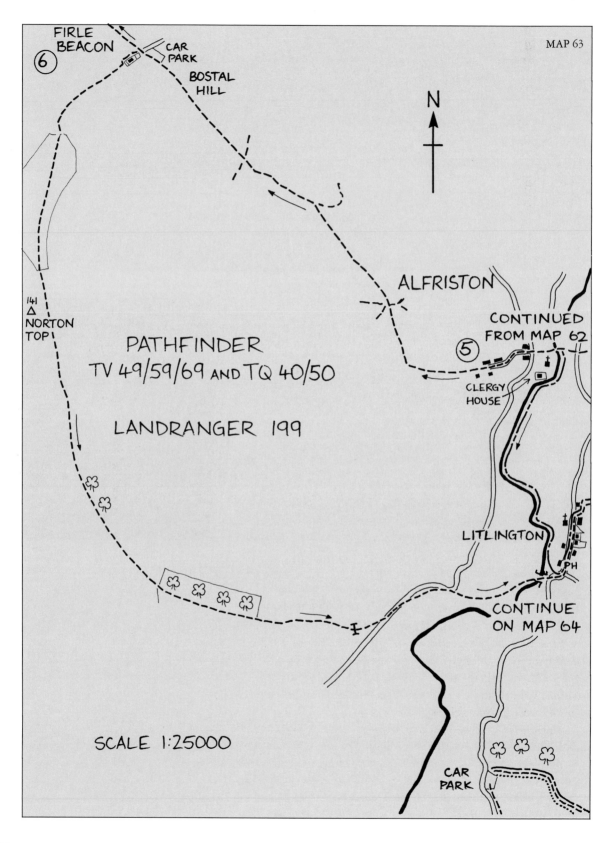

MAP 63

FIRLE
BEACON
⑥
CAR
PARK
BOSTAL
HILL

N

141
△
NORTON
TOP

ALFRISTON

CONTINUED
FROM MAP 62

⑤

CLERGY
HOUSE

PATHFINDER
TV 49/59/69 AND TQ 40/50

LANDRANGER 199

LITLINGTON

PH

CONTINUE
ON MAP 64

SCALE 1:25000

CAR
PARK

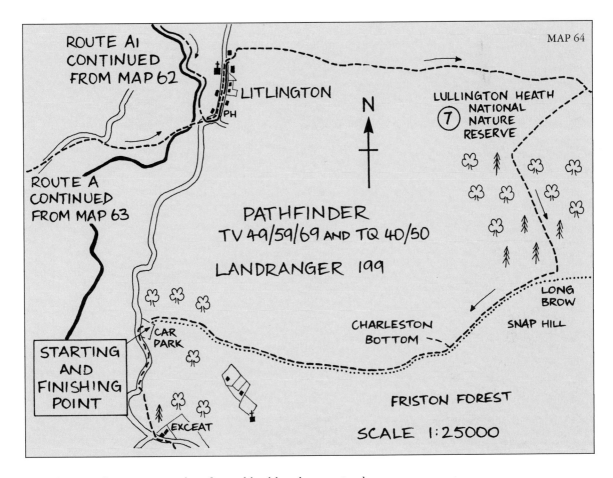

This fourteenth-century, timber-framed building has retained its original oak timbers and wattle and daub infilling. It was a typical medieval house with a central hall rising to the roof, but by the nineteenth century it had been converted into labourers' cottages and altered out of all recognition. It has been carefully restored.

6 *Firle Beacon*

Bostal is the Sussex name for a road or track that ascends the steep scarp slope of the Downs.

Firle Beacon and the village of Firle far below derive their name from an old English word meaning 'oak tree'. From the lofty 718 ft (219 m) Beacon there are extensive views over Mount Caburn and Glynde to the Ashdown Forest.

7 *Lullington Heath National Nature Reserve*

Lullington Heath National Nature Reserve was established in 1954 to conserve one of the largest areas of chalk heath remaining in Great Britain. Chalk heath develops where acid, sandy soil overlies the alkaline chalk. This allows the acid-loving plants like heather to thrive among the more characteristic Downland plants. Lack of grazing meant that tall grasses

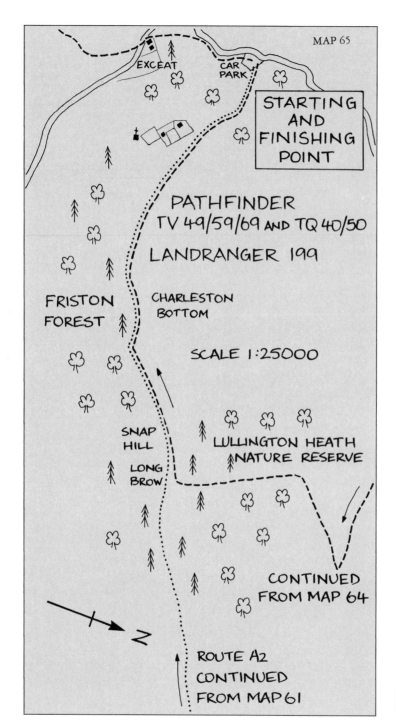

MAP 65

EXCEAT

CAR PARK

STARTING AND FINISHING POINT

PATHFINDER
TV 49/59/69 AND TQ 40/50

LANDRANGER 199

FRISTON FOREST

CHARLESTON BOTTOM

SCALE 1:25000

SNAP HILL

LONG BROW

LULLINGTON HEATH
NATURE RESERVE

CONTINUED FROM MAP 64

N

ROUTE A2
CONTINUED FROM MAP 61

The Seven Sisters.

and gorse had invaded the heathland but with grazing reintroduced by the NCC some grassland has been reinstated and the scrub kept low. Grazing peaked in the eighteenth and nineteenth centuries and many dew ponds were constructed to provide water for the stock.

APPENDICES

Access for the Walker

The walker enjoying the countryside has both rights and responsibilities. These are set out in the Countryside Access Charter published by the Countryside Commission and given below.

The 1949 National Parks and Access to the Countryside Act required County Councils in England and Wales to prepare definitive maps showing all public rights of way. These paths are classified either as public footpaths over which there is a right on foot only; bridleways for walkers, horse riders and cyclists, or a third category variously known as RUPPS (roads used as public paths) or CRBs (carriage roads mainly used as bridleways where in addition motor vehicles and horse drawn carriages have right-of-access). The 1981 Wildlife and Countryside Act modified the procedures laid down for the production of the definitive map and required that it should be continually updated. It also required RUPPS/CRB's to be reclassified to resolve uncertainties created by earlier legislation.

The inclusion of a right of way on the definitive map is conclusive evidence that it exists in law. County, District and Borough Council offices hold copies of the definitive map for their area and these can be inspected by the public. Occasionally these maps are displayed on Parish notice boards.

Paths can be diverted or less frequently extinguished as a result of Public Path Diversion or Extinguishment Orders. New paths can also be added to the map as a result of Dedication Agreements or Map Modification Orders when new evidence of use comes to light. The network therefore is not static.

Public rights of way are shown on Ordnance Survey Pathfinder, 1:25000, and Landranger, 1:50000, maps. Understandably, it is some years before the legal changes to the network find their way on to new additions of the OS maps but,

increasingly, legal changes are being well waymarked on site and notices erected to help the walker.

In the Downs and Weald there is continual pressure for development, and this creates the most rapid changes affecting public rights of way. The most intense pressure is around the towns and villages and the expanding road network.

Local Authorities own many Open Spaces over which the public have a right of access on foot and they may also manage privately-owned land under Access Agreements. The majority of land owned by the National Trust has open access and this includes many popular viewpoints. National Trust land and forest walks over Forestry Commission land are shown on the latest Ordnance Survey maps but other Open Spaces cannot be identified from them.

Landowners and land managers have a duty to ensure that rights of way are not obstructed and are reinstated after ploughing. The walker, too, has responsibilities enshrined in the Country Code. Dogs roaming at large over fields, woods and heaths are probably the greatest single cause of conflict in the countryside. Friendly, playful dogs can frighten sheep and deer and cause them to abort. In spring, they disturb ground-nesting birds and can destroy their eggs and chicks and occasionally fawns and lambs are killed. A well-disciplined dog on a lead or at heel is no threat to wildlife but one that runs loose is a menace.

There is no wild country in the Downs and Weald and few neglected areas. The land is managed for agriculture, horticulture and forestry as well as for conservation and access. It is a working environment and there are many, often conflicting, pressures upon it. Tolerance and understanding are needed on all sides.

Countryside Access Charter

YOUR RIGHTS OF WAY ARE

Public footpaths—on foot only. Sometimes way-marked in yellow

Bridleways—on foot, horseback and pedal cycle. Sometimes waymarked in blue

Byways (usually old roads), most 'Roads Used as Public Paths' and, of course, public roads—all traffic.

Use maps, signs and waymarks. Ordnance Survey Pathfinder and Landranger maps show most public rights of way.

ON RIGHTS OF WAY YOU CAN

Take a pram, pushchair or wheelchair if practicable

Take a dog (on a lead or under close control)

Take a short route round an illegal obstruction or remove it sufficiently to get past.

YOU HAVE A RIGHT TO GO FOR RECREATION TO

Public parks and open spaces—on foot

Most commons near older towns and cities—on foot and sometimes on horseback

Private land where the owner has a formal agreement with the local authority.

IN ADDITION YOU CAN USE BY LOCAL OR ESTABLISHED CUSTOM OR CONSENT, BUT ASK FOR ADVICE IF YOU'RE UNSURE

Many areas of open country like moorland, fell and coastal areas, especially those of the National Trust and some commons

Some woods and forests, especially those owned by the Forestry Commission

Country Parks and picnic sites

Most beaches

Canal towpaths

Some private paths and tracks. Consent sometimes extends to riding horses and pedal cycles.

FOR YOUR INFORMATION

County councils and London boroughs maintain and record rights of way, and register commons

Obstruction, dangerous animals, harassment and misleading signs on rights of way are illegal and you should report them to the county council

Paths across fields can be ploughed, but must normally be reinstated within two weeks

Landowners can require you to leave land to which you have no right of access

Motor vehicles are normally permitted only on roads, byways and some 'Roads Used as Public Paths'

Follow any local byelaws.

AND, WHEREVER YOU GO, FOLLOW THE COUNTRY CODE

Enjoy the countryside and respect its life and work

Guard against all risk of fire

Fasten all gates

Keep your dogs under close control

Keep to public paths across farmland

Use gates and stiles to cross fences, hedges and walls

Leave livestock, crops and machinery alone

Take your litter home

Help to keep all water clean

Protect wildlife, plants and trees

Take special care on country roads

Make no unnecessary noise.

This Charter is for practical guidance in England and Wales only.

Giving a Grid Reference

Giving a grid reference is an excellent way of 'pin-pointing' a feature, such as a church or hilltop on an Ordnance Survey map.

Grid lines, which are used for this purpose, are shown on the 1:25 000 Pathfinder and 1:50 000 Landranger maps produced by the Ordnance Survey; these are the maps most commonly used by walkers. They are the thin blue lines (one kilometre apart) going vertically and horizontally across the map producing a network of small squares. Each line, whether vertical or horizontal, is given a number from 00 to 99, with the sequence repeating itself every 100 lines. The 00 lines are slightly thicker than the others thus producing large squares with sides made up of 100 small squares and thus representing 100 kilometres. Each of these large squares is identified by two letters. The entire network of lines covering the British Isles, excluding Ireland, is called the National Grid.

Giving a grid reference

This shows a corner of an Ordnance Survey 1:50 000 Landranger map which contains a Youth Hostel. Using this map, the method of determining a grid reference is as follows:

Step 1

Holding the map in the normal upright position, note the number of the 'vertical' grid line to the left of the hostel. This is 72.

Step 2

Now imagine that the space between this grid line and the adjacent one to the right of the hostel is divided into ten equal divisions (the diagram on the right does this for you). Estimate the number of these 'tenths' that the hostel lies to the right of the left-hand grid line. This is 8. Add this to the number found in Step 1 to make 728.

Step 3

Note the number of the grid line below the hostel and add it on to the number obtained above. This is 21, so that the number becomes 72821.

Step 4

Repeat Step 2 for the space containing the hostel, but now in a vertical direction. The final number to be added is 5, making 728215. This is called a six-figure grid reference. This, coupled with the number or name of the appropriate Landranger or Outdoor Leisure map, will enable the Youth Hostel to be found.

A full grid reference will also include the identification of the appropriate 100 kilometre square of the National Grid; for example, SU 728215. This information is given in the margin of each map.

Addresses of Useful Organizations

East Sussex County Council
Rights of Way
Phoenix Causeway
Lewes
East Sussex
BN 1UE
Lewes (0273) 481000

Kent County Council
Rights of Way
Springfield
Maidstone
Kent
ME14 2LQ
Maidstone (0622) 671411

Surrey County Council
Rights of Way
Highway House
21 Chessington Road
West Ewell
Epsom
Surrey
01-541 7272

West Sussex County Council
Rights of Way
County Hall
Chichester
West Sussex
PO19 1RL
Chichester (0243) 777100

Countryside Commission
John Dower House
Crescent Place
Cheltenham
Gloucestershire GL50 3RA
Cheltenham (0242) 521381

English Heritage
Keysign House
429 Oxford Street
London
W1R 2HD
01-355 1303

National Trust (Southern Region)
Polesden Lacey
Great Bookham
Dorking
Surrey
RH5 6BD
Bookham (0372) 56977

The Ramblers' Association
1/5 Wandsworth Road
London SW8 2XX
01-582 6878

Long Distance Walkers Association
Membership Secretary
Kevin Uzzell
7 Ford Drive
Yarnfield
Stone
Staffordshire
ST15 0RP

Nature Conservancy Council
Northminster House
Northminster Road
Peterborough
Cambridgeshire
PE1 1UA
Peterborough (0733) 40345

Kent Trust For Nature Conservation
Bower Mount Road
Maidstone
Kent
Maidstone (0622) 59017

Surrey Wildlife Trust
Old School
Pirbright
Woking
Surrey
GU 24 0JN
Woking (0483) 797575

Sussex Wildlife Trust
Woods Mill
Henfield
West Sussex
BN5 9SD
Henfield (0273) 492630

Woodland Trust
Westgate
Grantham
Lincs
NG31 6LL
Grantham (0476) 74297

Ordnance Survey Map Suppliers
Edward Stanford Ltd
12–14 Long Acre
London WC2E 9LP
01-836 1321

GUIDE BOOKS

Downs Link

Surrey County Council
Rights of Way
Highway House
21 Chessington Road
West Ewell
Epsom
Surrey
KT22 7HN
01-541 7272

Greensand Way

Surrey:

Surrey County Council
Rights of Way
Highway House
21 Chessington Road
West Ewell
Epsom
Surrey
KT22 7HN
01-541 7272

Kent:

Ramblers Association
42 Waldron Drive
Loose
Maidstone
Kent ME15 9TH

North Downs Way and
South Downs Way:

HMSO Publications
PMIC Atlantic House
Holborn Viaduct
London EC1P 1BN
01-873 0011

Sussex Border Path and Wealdway:

Ben Perkins
11 Old London Road
Brighton
Sussex
BN1 8XR

Vanguard Way:

Vanguards Rambling Club
109 Selsdon Park Road
Croydon
CR2 8JJ

INDEX

Place names and sites of interest only are included.